NEW DIRECTIONS
FOR CHILD
DEVELOPMENT

Number 11 • 1981

NEW DIRECTIONS FOR CHILD DEVELOPMENT

A Quarterly Sourcebook
William Damon, Editor-in-Chief

Number 11, 1981

Developmental Perspectives on Child Maltreatment

Ross Rizley
Dante Cicchetti
Guest Editors

Jossey-Bass Inc., Publishers
San Francisco • Washington • London

DEVELOPMENTAL PERSPECTIVES ON CHILD MALTREATMENT
New Directions for Child Development
Number 11, 1981
     Ross Rizley, Dante Cicchetti, Guest Editors

New Directions for Child Development (publication number
USPS 494-090) is published quarterly by Jossey-Bass Inc., Publishers.
Subscriptions are available at the regular rate for institutions,
libraries, and agencies of $30 for one year. Individuals may
subscribe at the special professional rate of $18 for one year.

Correspondence:
Subscriptions, single-issue orders, change of address notices,
undelivered copies, and other correspondence should be sent to
New Directions Subscriptions, Jossey-Bass Inc., Publishers,
433 California Street, San Francisco, California 94104.

Editorial correspondence should be sent to the Editor-in-Chief,
William Damon, Department of Psychology, Clark University,
Worcester, Massachusetts 01610.

Library of Congress Catalogue Card Number LC 80-84255

International Standard Serial Number ISSN 0195-2269

International Standard Book Number ISBN 87589-801-7

Cover design by Willi Baum

Manufactured in the United States of America

Contents

Editors' Notes

For years unrecognized as the pervasive social problem we now know it to be, child maltreatment has recently received increased scientific and public attention. Scores of professional papers have reviewed the state of our knowledge of this important problem. Nevertheless, we know next to nothing about child maltreatment. We have very little systematically collected, scientifically acceptable information about the antecedents, manifestations, sequelae (developmental, social, legal, and so on), treatment responses, or intergenerational transmission of maltreatment. Moreover, the existing literature is riddled with the views, opinions, and idiosyncratic orientations of a variety of disciplines, including psychology, pediatrics, psychiatry, social work, and law. While there are attempts to present comprehensive models of maltreatment, generally these efforts represent only a pretheoretical orientation and a useful but preliminary "language system." Often they are silent about one or more of the issues of etiology, transmission, sequelae, or differential treatment response.

Moreover, research in the area has been plagued with methodological problems and theoretical misconceptions, resulting in an accumulation of diverse and even contradictory findings, which have contributed less than they might have to the clarification of the problem or the identification of its causes or consequences. We know very little about the efficacy of therapeutic programs, about the types of professionals who might most effectively provide services, or about the type of professional training needed. In addition, while many prescriptions have been suggested for eradicating the conditions that encourage child maltreatment, there are few substantive empirical data on which to base social policies to address the problem. The most salient fact that may be gleaned from the literature in this area is that child maltreatment is not a unitary construct with a simple definition, a single etiology, or a single set of consequences, but a complex, multifactored set of syndromes with multiple manifestations, etiologies, and possible sequelae. If we are going to progress in unraveling the complex etiologies of maltreatment and in understanding the adaptation of maltreated children, this paucity of critical information must be remedied.

We are committed to the idea that research on child maltreatment must reflect the complexity of the phenomenon itself. Theories and research strategies must recognize that there are four types of heterogeneity: in type of maltreatment, in etiology, in sequelae, and in treatment response. Moreover, research must utilize sophisticated and multicontextual developmental measurement techniques and complex developmental models. The unifying theme to this volume is the need for increasing sophistication in our research techniques and theoretical notions regarding children and their maltreatment. We must acknowledge the complexity of the phenomenon before we can progress in our understanding of it.

The chapters in this volume of *New Directions for Child Development* share a common commitment to the notion that theory and techniques derived from developmental psychology and developmental biology can contribute greatly to our understanding, treatment, and prevention of child maltreatment.

J. Lawrence Aber, III and Edward Zigler argue forcefully in the first chapter for the need to consider developmental factors in defining and classifying child maltreatment.

Chapters Two through Four describe ongoing, large-scale projects funded by the National Center on Child Abuse and Neglect, each of which is concerned with the developmental sequelae and etiologic aspects of child maltreatment. While each adopts a somewhat different theoretical and measurement stance, each utilizes a complex multifactored approach to the study of this difficult social problem. Chapter Two describes our longitudinal study at Harvard University, examining the etiology, intergenerational transmission, and developmental sequelae of maltreatment. Chapter Three describes the cross-sectional and longitudinal studies in Pennsylvania conducted by Roy and Ellen Herrenkohl, focusing on the antecedents and sequelae of maltreatment. Chapter Four describes the longitudinal, predictive investigation conducted by Byron Egeland and Alan Sroufe in Minnesota, a prospective study of primiparous, high-risk mothers and their infants through the first two years of life. Each of these three projects adopts a developmental framework, each attempts to use sophisticated assessments of child development and developmental sequelae, and each acknowledges in one way or another the enormous complexity of the phenomena subsumed under the rubric of child maltreatment.

The final chapter by Martin Daly and Margo Wilson places the issues of maltreatment in a broader, evolutionary, transgenerational and transcultural perspective. We asked Daly and Wilson to discuss the significance of child maltreatment from a sociobiological, developmental perspective, and their paper reminds us that the problem of child maltreatment transcends any particular time or culture, and may be understood from the perspective of evolutionary theory.

The order of guest editors' names was decided by a flip of a coin. Both contributed equally to the content and preparation of this journal. We wish to acknowledge the support of Grant #90–C–1929 from the National Center on Child Abuse and Neglect, Administration for Children, Youth and Families, Office of Human Development.

Ross Rizley
Dante Cicchetti
Guest Editors

Ross Rizley is an assistant professor of psychology and social relations at Harvard University where he is co-director of the Developmental Risk Research Project and the Harvard Child Maltreatment Project.

Dante Cicchetti is an assistant professor of psychology and social relations at Harvard University where he is co-director of the Developmental Risk Research Project and the Harvard Child Maltreatment Project.

Conflict among definitions of child maltreatment abounds. Diagnostic, sociological, legal, and research approaches each focus on a different aspect of the phenomenon as the defining factor. Improved definitions require careful analysis of objectives for defining child maltreatment and a consideration of the developmental nature of the phenomenon.

Developmental Considerations in the Definition of Child Maltreatment

J. Lawrence Aber III
Edward Zigler

The State of the Art

Child maltreatment in all its various forms is an ancient phenomenon (Radbill, 1974). Bakan (1971) eloquently describes its prebiblical and Old Testament heritage. Giovannoni and Becerra (1979) and Ross (1980) trace its unique expressions in nineteenth and twentieth century England and America, and document the evolution of efforts to combat and control the problems.

Nonetheless, formal attempts to define child maltreatment are a modern development that can be linked in part to the professionalization of certain social functions. Modern culture has witnessed the unprecedented growth of law and the social and health sciences as means of negotiating conflicts that at one time were settled by religion or tribal and folk custom. These professional

The senior author wishes gratefully to acknowledge the Bush Foundation of St. Paul, Minnesota and Department of Health, Education and Welfare Grant No. 90-C-1929 on the etiology, transmission, and sequelae of child maltreatment for their support during the preparation of this chapter.

disciplines, administered by institutions, require inclusion and exclusion rules to decide what events or conditions constitute an appropriate "case" for their jurisdiction in a way not necessary for a priest or local patriarch.

Because a particular constellation of events or conditions can meet more than one set of inclusion and exclusion rules on different levels of analysis, the development of rules to define "cases" carries with it the possibility of discovering new relationships among diverse phenomena previously considered unrelated. Inclusion and exclusion rules of the various professions also create the conditions for debates about which set of rules should prevail. The modern history of formal attempts to define child maltreatment illustrates such a debate.

Medical Diagnostic Definition. In 1946, a pediatric radiologist named John Caffey began to publish accounts of bone fractures to children of unspecified cause (Caffey, 1946). During the 1950s, investigators speculated that these fractures might be caused by accident, carelessness or parental irresponsibility or immaturity (Pfohl, 1977; Ross, 1980). The first formal definition of child maltreatment, proposed by C. Henry Kempe and his colleagues in the early 1960s, grew out of this tradition. The radiological evidence of a history of multiple and repeated fractures to children coupled with the fact that parents could not adequately explain the cause of the fractures, led Kempke to conclude that some parents intentionally inflict injuries upon their own children. He coined the term "battered child syndrome" to describe this constellation of events and conditions (Kempe and others, 1962).

The purposes and processes of classifying a case as "battered child syndrome" constitutes a medical diagnostic definition of child maltreatment (for further discussion see Giovannoni and Becerra, 1979, pp. 20–23). Kempe's desire to develop a diagnostic approach to defining child maltreatment seemed to stem from the general success of the use of diagnoses in the medical sciences. The aim of a medical diagnostic definition is to identify a pathological process or condition underlying a symptom pattern in a way that enables a therapeutic intervention. If a symptom pattern can be described but the underlying pathology cannot yet be identified, the diagnosis is considered incomplete. Kempe's definition of child abuse served the purpose of a diagnosis in which the underlying pathology is identified (characteristics of the abuser), not just the surface symptom (the act of maltreatment itself).

The symptom functions as a sign pointing to the underlying pathology, the diagnostician searches within the individual patient for the problem producing the symptom. Since the ultimate goal of a diagnosis is therapeutic intervention, the diagnostic approach implies an individual, case-level response to the pathology.

A diagnostic approach also makes it theoretically possible to identify the underlying pathology before the expression of symptoms. In the case of child maltreatment. Kempe and his colleagues believed that on the basis of parental characteristics diagnosticians would be able to identify potential abusers before they actually abused their children. Thus, the basic nosology of a medical diagnostic schema for defining child maltreatment is a dichotomous classification of parents as potentially abusive: yes or no?

The medical diagnostic approach enjoyed nearly a decade of supremacy in defining child maltreatment. In the 1970s, the sociological, legal, and research approaches described below called into question the basic philosophy of the diagnostic approach. But even accepting medical diagnosis as a legitimate method for defining child maltreatment, the Kempe effort is vulnerable to criticisms leveled at a related field of medicine, the field of psychiatric diagnosis (Zigler and Phillips, 1961).

A diagnostic definition is a form of classification system. "A diagnosis is a basic classificatory enterprise to be viewed as essentially the practice of taxonomy which is characteristic of all science" (Zigler and Phillips, 1961, p. 607). At an early stage of development of a scientific field, a classification system may include only descriptive characteristics which define class membership. Later, the system may also include broad ranging attributes or correlates of class membership, those valid statements that can be made of phenomena once they are classified.

Zigler and Phillips criticized scholars of psychiatric diagnoses for failing to distinguish between class characteristics and class correlates. In a similar view, the authors advised scholars that reliability of a classification system based on descriptive class characteristics should take priority over the validity of the system based upon class correlates. A classification system can be reliable without being valid for some purposes, but it can never be valid for any purpose without being reliable. Without reliability, there is no true classification system.

Scientists and clinicians can agree on reliable, descriptive characteristics of a class without agreeing on all its correlates or even on the types of correlates most important to the classification system. The types of statements one may wish to make about class correlates are many and include statements about etiology, sequelae, treatment response and prognosis. Assertions by proponents of particular classification schemes that certain correlates accompany class membership can be subjected to empirical test. If the hypothesized correlates are not found to be related to class membership, then revision of the classification system is in order.

In light of these critical remarks on the state of psychiatric diagnoses, it appears that Kempe failed to clearly distinguish between class characteristics and class correlates in his diagnostic scheme. He tied physical injury to children, a descriptive characteristic with high reliability, to intentionality and parental characteristics, best considered as hypothesized correlates, as defining factors of the battered child syndrome. By confusing class characteristics and class correlates, Kempe also failed to address separately the issues of the reliability and validity of the classification system.

Rather than having failed to distinguish class characteristics and class correlates, Kempe may have viewed the child maltreatment field as sufficiently advanced to leap into a classification system that included both descriptive characteristics as well as broad-ranging attributes of class membership. If so, Kempe apparently considered the following issues as settled: first, the question of the most important types of class correlates to include in the classification system, etiologic factors; second, the most important etiologic factor, characteristics of the parents. Other points of view on these two issues have emerged in the last ten years. As will be described below, the issue of the most important type of correlates to include in a classification system for defining child maltreatment is now a matter of policy debate between diagnosticians and lawyers who have mounted compelling arguments for considering sequelae, not etiology, as the most important correlates. And the issue of the most important etiologic factor is now a matter of empirical debate among researchers from various disciplines. Kempe's premature closure of the policy debate over the most important correlates and the empirical debate on the most important etiologic factor to include in a classification scheme has led to a premature and potentially dangerous effort to develop risk profiles of parent characteristics for use in predicting which parents may abuse their children (see Cicchetti and Aber, 1980, for a critique of this predictive approach).

Sociological Definition. The definition most consciously at odds with the medical diagnostic definition is the sociological definition based on the concept of social deviance. A sophisticated version of this definition which has in turn supported the most fruitful empirical research on the process of defining child abuse cases has been proposed by Giovannoni and Becerra (1979). Better known sociological definitions of child maltreatment, for example, the works of Gil (1970) and Gelles (1975; 1980) are not discussed at this point for two reasons. First, they focus primarily on physical violence to children, not on the broad spectrum of acts and conditions which qualify as child maltreatment. Second, they use their definitions of child abuse to conduct studies of the incidence, prevalence and social structural determinants of physical violence to children, not to study the process by which child maltreatment is defined. The sociological definition of Giovannoni and Becerra is best described by contrasting it to the diagnostic definition to which it is a reaction. The basic aim of this definition is labeling and controlling social deviance, which stands in marked contrast to the aims of identifying and curing pathology. The focus of the sociological definition is on the act of maltreatment itself, not on the characteristics of the maltreaters. This definition concerns itself with more than just physical abuse; it includes all forms of child maltreatment. Unlike the basic evaluative question asked by the diagnostician about a case, namely "is this parent potentially abusive, yes or no," the question posed by the sociologist is "how serious is this form of maltreatment and how much does it need to be controlled?" The process of defining child maltreatment is understood as social-judgmental, not clinical-scientific. And because maltreatment is not considered to be a problem that resides within the individual abuser, but instead is thought to be a socially defined problem, the sociological definition implies social solutions (Gelles, 1975).

Although the sociological definition represents an important alternative to the diagnostic definition in many respects, it too suffers from certain inherent limits (Alvy, 1975). Chief among them is the assumption that the judgment by social agents of the seriousness of the type of maltreatment corresponds with the actual severity of the specific harm to the child. The sociological definition ignores the possibility that regardless of how society defines certain parental acts, they may or may not result in damage to the child's social, emotional, cognitive, or physical development. To recognize that child maltreatment is in part defined by social agents in a social context where role expectations of parental behavior in a certain culture are violated should not discourage efforts to understand the meaning of maltreatment from the child's perspective.

For instance, Giovannoni and Becerra (1979) found that professionals and community representatives alike consider sexual abuse to be the second most serious general type of child maltreatment, ranking just below physical injury and very well ahead of emotional maltreatment, ranked fifth. Even on the behavioral level, "child openly rejected; siblings obviously preferred," usually a chronic condition, was rated as less serious than "sexual abuse/molestation of child by a (nonparental) adult," usually a single episode (Giovannoni and Becerra, 1979, p. 218). The disturbing aspect of these findings is not that adults consider any type of sexual abuse to be a more serious form of maltreatment than even most harmful forms of parental rejection; it is that the social labeling approach to defining child maltreatment cannot treat the question of relative harm to the child as an empirical issue. To the extent that the sociological definition views the definitional process as purely social-judgmental and fails to consider the empirical effects of the act on the child, it makes an arbitrary and unnecessary choice to view child maltreatment as a social symbolic phenomenon, not an act with real, organic, developmental consequences to the child.

Legal Definition. In reaction to the inadequacies of both the medical diagnostic and the sociological definitions of child maltreatment as guidelines for state intervention into family life, a set of legal definitions was developed by Wald and his colleagues for the Juvenile Justice Standards Project (1977). Curiously, it is the first work to explicitly state that standards such as the two that follow should serve as the criteria for defining child maltreatment: "A child has suffered or there is a substantial risk that a child will imminently suffer, a physical harm . . . or serious physical injury," or "A child is suffering serious emotional damage . . . and the child's parents are not willing to provide treatment for him/her" (Juvenile Justice Standards Project, 1977, pp. 10–11). This legal model offers an important corrective by suggesting that harm to the child, not characteristics of the abusers or the act of mistreatment, should serve as the determining factor in defining child maltreatment.

In addition to this focus on harm to the child, the standards include four other major improvements in the substance and process of defining child maltreatment. First, the standards recognize that different legal objectives require different definitions to guide decision making. Hence, the standards propose that coercive court intervention be directed at the "endangered child" (the definition of which includes emotional damage), while mandatory reporting to state social service agencies be restricted to reporting on the "abused child" (the definition of which includes physical injury only) (Juvenile Justice Standards Project, 1977, p. 10).

Second, the standards correctly argue that clear definitions of child maltreatment must be based upon explicit statements of value preferences. They are premised on such general principles as the presumption of family autonomy in childrearing, and designing an intervention system that promotes a child's need for a continuous and stable living environment and that reflects developmental differences among children of various ages (Juvenile Justice Standards Project, 1977, pp. 37–48). Thus, when one evaluates the adequacy of a definition of child maltreatment, one should consider the objectives of the definition and the value preferences associated with the objectives as well as the technical ability of the definition in meeting the objectives. If the objectives lack clarity and if great political controversy surrounds the values underlying the objectives, the definition's technical merit is likely to suffer.

The third advance made by the legal definition over the diagnostic and sociological definitions is its ability to begin to tackle the problem of intentionality. As a practical issue, the concept of parents' intentions very much influences the judgments of decision makers about whether a constellation of events or conditions constitutes a case of child maltreatment. If a child is injured "on purpose," not "by accident," the act is much more likely to be included as child maltreatment. Yet, because of the legal and clinical-scientific difficulty of ascertaining intentionality, some have suggested abandoning the concept as part of a definition of child maltreatment.

The standards cut through this problem by requiring that a specific harm, or a substantial risk of imminent harm, first be documented in order to include a case as child maltreatment. In this scheme, the problem of intentionality functions as a secondary exclusionary rule. If the harm can be found to be accidental, or as a result of conditions not created by the parents or the parents' failure to adequately supervise the child, the specific harm can be excluded as a case of maltreatment.

A final improvement of the legal definition is its insistence that general harm to the child be documented by evidence. Thus, physical harm must cause "disfigurement, impairment of bodily functioning, or other serious injury" (p. 51). Emotional damage must be "evidenced by severe anxiety, depression, withdrawal, or untoward aggressive behavior toward self or others" (p. 55). A social science corollary to this legal principle of requiring evidence of harm is the research principle of operationalizing a construct so that empirical research can be conducted and so that statements about the construct can be verified or falsified (Meehl, 1978; Popper, 1959). This principle of operationalism to allow verification or falsification is no less critical to legal and clinical decision making than to good empirical research about child maltreatment.

Research Definitions. The principal functions of the diagnostic, sociological and legal definitions of child maltreatment were to guide clinical, social, and legal decision making. A final set of definitions has developed over the last decade out of research efforts to explain child maltreatment, especially its nature, causes, and effects, and to evaluate programmatic efforts to cure, control, or prevent the problem.

There are two common strategies for defining maltreatment for research purposes. The first, using a child abuse report to a state agency as an operational definition, has been discussed elsewhere (Aber, 1980; Zigler, 1980). Reliance on a report to a state agency suffers the obvious problems of questionable reliability and validity. First, the criteria justifying a report vary from jurisdiction to jurisdiction, raising the problem of comparability of defininitions. Second, the criteria to be used by child care professionals, family members, and neighbors to report cases of suspected maltreatment are so vaguely articulated in statutory law and in social agency regulations that they are applied very unevenly by reporters, thus reducing their reliability. Even among professionals required to investigate reports and screen cases according to the criteria, the reliability of judgments is very low, due largely to the vagueness of the classification system employed. As importantly, in many states the criteria used to justify a report of child abuse bear little relation to the issues that endanger a child's health, safety, or welfare. Thus, the validity of a report to an agency as a definition of child maltreatment is called into question.

The second strategy, defining child maltreatment in very narrow and explicit behavioral terms is best exemplified in the ground-breaking sociological research of Gelles (1980) on the prevalence and incidence of physical violence between spouse and spouse and between parent and child in America. Although Gelles is interested in understanding the broad social structural correlates of physical violence to children, he has chosen to focus on the one sub-type among many types of maltreatment that is easiest to define in explicit, behavioral terms. This approach has met with some success in its major goal: to increase the scientific reliability of the classification. But the narrowness of the definition has limited its appeal to other researchers.

Despite its lack of attention to the definitional problem per se, another research tradition based upon the theoretical work of Bronfenbrenner (1977) is worth mentioning because it highlights an important aspect of the phenomenon which has not been adequately addressed by the previous definitions. By focusing on the ecology of human development, researchers in this tradition have mounted important theoretical (Belsky, 1980) and empirical (Garbarino, 1976; Garbarino and Crouter, 1978) studies of family/environment transactions and the role of social-environmental supports and stresses in increasing or decreasing the risk of child maltreatment in a particular family or community.

The major point of these studies is that the ontogenetic development of parents and children cannot account for all the data presently available on the causes of child maltreatment. Because parent/child interactions vary so greatly with ecological context, the social-familial environment (named by Bronfenbrenner the "exosystem") and the larger historical-cultural environment (the "macrosystem") must also be considered. Thus, developmental ecology implicitly poses the question of whether the environment should also be considered a determining factor in defining child maltreatment.

Status of the Debate

Underlying the many apparent differences among these four modern approaches to defining child maltreatment, two major issues can be identified on which most of the debates seem to focus. These issues offer important clues about how to bring order to the confusion surrounding efforts to formally define child maltreatment.

Broad versus Narrow Definition. Perhaps the issue most heatedly debated among the advocates of the various approaches concerns the scope of those events or conditions that a definition of child maltreatment should cover. The debate centers upon the relative merits of developing and employing broad versus narrow definitions. The medical-diagnostic definition of "battered child" and the legal definition of "abused child" described above are examples of narrowly drawn definitions of child maltreatment, restricted as they are to documentable instances of physical injury to the child. The sociological definition cast the broadest net of the four definitions, including not only physical injury but also seven other subtypes of maltreatment ranging from emotional mistreatment and sexual abuse of the child to moral and legal problems of the parent to inadequate physical environment. Between these two ends of the spectrum lies the legal definition of "endangered child," a definition that focuses on more than just physical harm to the child but specifies only four other subtypes of harm (emotional damage, sexual abuse, parent unwilling to provide medical treatment necessary to prevent serious physical harm, and parental encouragement or approval to child committing a delinquent act) in a fashion less inclusive than the sociological definition and requiring much more concrete evidence to document.

Subsumed under this general issue of the breadth of definition is a series of closely related subissues (see Table 1). Proponents of narrow definitions of child maltreatment tend to view the problem as caused by individuals and so requiring case-level solutions. The general social aim of the narrow definition is to treat or understand the most severe cases of maltreatment; the specific objective of the definition is to provide guidelines for intervention and decision making. Advocates of the broader definitions, on the other hand, tend to proffer social structural theories of the causes of child maltreatment and social solutions to the problem. The general social aim of the broad definitions points toward improving the lives of all children in society by reducing hindrances to their development. Thus, the specific objective of definitions is to further studies of and action on the continuum of parental behaviors and environmental conditions that hinder optimal child development.

Advocating broad or narrow definitions also seems to carry with it political and scientific ramifications that are not immediately apparent. Politically, use of a broad definition generally creates greater eligibility and demands for social services and consequently higher caseloads. Narrow definitions restrict eligibility for services and reduce caseloads. Broad definitions seem to increase the discretion of clinical and legal decision makers in applying the definition to a particular family and so they are sometimes labeled liberal or

Table 1. The Debate Over the Proper Scope of a Definition of Child Maltreatment

	Narrow Definition	*Broad Definition*
Cause	Individual abuser	Social structure
Solution	Case level	Society level
Social Aim	To eliminate the most severe cases	To improve the lives of all children by reducing hindrances to their development
Objective of Definition	To guide intervention and decision making in individual cases	To study and act on a continuum of parental behaviors and environmental conditions that hinder optimal development

prointerventionist; narrow definitions are thought to limit the discretion of decision makers and consequently are libertarian or antiinterventionist. These political labels associated with support of narrow or broad definitions may prove to be more confusing than helpful. For example, a narrow definition does not have to restrict intake to voluntary services if it is used exclusively to make decisions about coercive intervention.

Scientifically, narrow definitions tend to be easier to operationalize and hence to use to construct clear, explicit inclusion and exclusion rules and decision-making criteria; broader definitions are more difficult to operationalize and so diminish the clarity of decision rules based upon them.

It is important to state that these two groups of subissues associated with support for broad or narrow definitions only tend to go together. There are important exceptions to these tendencies as illustrated by the example of a narrow definition not necessarily restricting eligibility for voluntary services. Similarly, the Gelles approach to child maltreatment focuses on social structural causes of child abuse but restricts its investigations to the causes of physical violence only. Nonetheless, the debate between advocates of narrow and broad definitions seems to capture many of the differences that exist among the various approaches to defining child maltreatment.

Epistemological Priority of Each Definition. The second major issue debated among the four approaches to defining child maltreatment concerns the choice of the determining factor for the definition. Contrast the point of view of the legal approach expressed by Michael Wald and his colleagues (Juvenile Justice Standards Project, 1977, p. 9): "Coercive state intervention should be premised upon specific harms that a child has suffered or is likely to suffer" with that of the distinguished developmental psychologist Mary Ainsworth (1980, pp. 44–45) expressing the views of the diagnostic approach: "The most difficult, and yet the most important, criterion for intervention is the identification of a parent as potentially abusing." The sociological definition offers a third choice of determining factor: the degree to which specific parental acts deviate from our culture's values of acceptable childrearing which in turn relates to our values regarding what constitutes a "good adult" (Giovannoni and Becerra, 1979, p. 4).

In short, each definitional scheme assigns epistemological priority to one variable among the many that together constitute the complex phenomenon of child maltreatment (see Table 2). Among the four approaches to definitions of maltreatment reviewed above, only the research tradition of the ecology of human development assigns an explicit status to the four variables of parent characteristics (P), act of maltreatment (A), child effects (C), and environmental conditions (E); not for the purposes of definition but rather to develop a research framework capable of integrating various research findings (Belsky, 1980).

Table 2. Epistemological Priorities Assigned by Each Approach

School of Definition	Determining Factor for Definition	
Medical–Diagnostic	Characteristics of Parent	(P)
Sociological	Acts of Maltreatment	(A)
Legal	Harms to the Child	(C)
Research	Environmental Conditions	(E)

It is not accidental that each approach to defining child maltreatment has been proposed by a different profession with a different set of institutional interests to protect and social aims to pursue: medical and mental health scientists and practitioners, social welfare theorists and social workers, legal scholars and lawyers, and research scientists in government and academia. Each professional group pursues various legitimate interests and aims important to society. The health science's role in curing pathology naturally and appropriately leads to an interest in diagnostic indicators; the bar's role in safeguarding the legal rights of children and their families leads to a desire to specify the types of harm to children that justify state intervention, and so on. Similarly, it is natural and appropriate for doctors to want a diagnostic assessment tool when the aspect of child maltreatment that they feel most competent to address is the problem of the abusing parents; analogously, lawyers hope for an established calculus of harms to the the child.

In other words, the interest that each profession shows in the defining factor of child maltreatment is related to the goals and objectives of the profession and its relative ability to exert leverage on some aspect of the problem. That professions wish to assign priority to variables that they feel some competence to address, natural as it is, nonetheless reminds us of Maslow's adage that if all you have is a hammer, you begin to approach every problem as if it were a nail. Thus, a problem arises when a profession assumes that because they are primarily interested in one facet of a complex problem in order to pursue their own legitimate social aim, then that aspect should acquire an epistemological priority over other aspects of the problem for the purposes of defining that problem.

Rethinking the Debate. Alternative approaches to defining child maltreatment have been described and the points of fundamental debate among the approaches have been outlined. At this point, a series of thorny questions pops up. How are we to rate the comparative value of these various definitions? Given that each seems to have its relative strengths and weaknesses, how are we to choose among them to respond to the pressing need for a common definition of maltreatment that will solve the problems of incomparable research studies, incompatible laws and social policies, and inconsistent legal and clinical decision making?

Clearly, major differences exist among the four definitions' premises, objectives, and primary foci. Are these differences irreconcilable, forcing us to ask the question of which single definition should prevail? Or is there a way of understanding these differences so that future definers of child maltreatment can capitalize on the strength of each definition and minimize its weaknesses in creating a new definitional schema?

An important first step in answering these questions is to critically examine the prevailing assumption that one common definition will suffice to pursue all the various social aims and objectives for which a definition is needed. Elsewhere, we have concluded that no one definition can logically fulfill all these purposes (see Ross and others, 1979; Ross and Zigler, 1980). We propose instead that a finite number of formal definitions of child maltreatment be developed and that each definition should be tailored to the major social aims and objectives for which it is intended. In other words, we need to differentiate definitions by social aim and objective.

At least three different sets of definitions to pursue three social aims are needed: first, *legal definitions* to guide legal decision making that would specify what acts or conditions justify initial state intervention into private family life (what justifies a report of maltreatment?), coercive state intervention (what justifies requiring families to receive services?), and termination of parental rights to custody; second, *case management definitions* to guide clinical decision making that would specify eligibility criteria for voluntary services and establish a baseline against which services are evaluated and clinical decisions about the families are made; and third, *research definitions* to guide scientific research that would provide the basis for studying lawful, causal relationships among four types of variables: parent characteristics, parental acts and behaviors, child characteristics and effects, and social and cultural environmental conditions (see Ross and others, 1979, for further discussion).

By recognizing the necessity of three different sets of definitions to pursue such different social aims, the debate between narrow and broad definitions can begin to be resolved. If the differences in social aims are made explicit, the value of narrow definitions to guide legal decision making and broad definitions to structure comprehensive empirical research programs can be asserted without any logical inconsistencies.

A second major step in reconciling the differences among the various definitions is to recognize that each definition carries with it a different theory of the basic nature of the phenomenon of child maltreatment. We have already discussed one aspect of theories, namely the epistemological priority they assign to one aspect of this complex phenomenon over others. A second aspect of the theories of the basic nature of child maltreatment is the implicit causal model of each definition, which we have diagrammed below (see Table 3). Not every example of a definition implies its corresponding causal model. But the bulk of work in each tradition is premised on these models.

Table 3. The Implied Causal Models of Each Definitional Approach

Approach to Definition	Priority Variable	Causal Direction	Secondary Variables
Medical–Diagnostic	Parent	$\longrightarrow$	Child
Legal	Child	$\longleftarrow$	Parent
Sociological	Act	$\longleftarrow$ / $\longrightarrow$	Parent / Child

While these different theories of the basic nature of child maltreatment are understandable on professional grounds, they are becoming increasingly untenable on scientific grounds. None of the causal models outlined above possess sufficient predictive or explanatory value to account for the wealth of empirical data that already exist on the nature, causes, and effects of child maltreatment (Belsky, 1980; Cicchetti, Taraldson and Egeland, 1978). Given this state of affairs, it is highly unlikely that any one of these models alone will prove rich enough to structure and guide empirical research or clinical and legal decision making in the near future.

We believe that a working model of the basic nature of child maltreatment would be inadequate without accounting for all four basic factors described individually by the various approaches, namely parent characteristics (P), act of maltreatment (A), child effects (C) and environmental factors (E). In addition, given the increasing evidence on the fundamental reciprocity of parent/child, child/environment, and parent/environment relations, we suggest that the issue of causal direction of relations be considered an open question and approached empirically, not dogmatically.

Undoubtedly some will argue that this unnecessarily complicates the already complex problem of developing adequate definitions of child maltreatment. How, it will be asked, can one possibly develop clear, operationalizable inclusion and exclusion rules to guide clinical and legal decision making and empirical research if we have to simultaneously consider four aspects or dimensions of the problem rather than one? The task seems formidable. But we consider the rewards to be well worth the effort because our own reading of the modern history of defining child maltreatment convinces us that it is by trying to sidestep the complexity of the phenomenon that we have encountered the biggest problems. In addition, the work of theoreticians and scholars like Belsky and Wald inspires us to believe that a definitional or explanatory schema that seems more complex over the short run can sometimes be more elegant and above all more useful over the long run, especially if it is based on assumptions that more closely mirror the basic nature of the phenomenon.

14

Developmental Considerations in Defining Child Maltreatment

We now turn to another aspect of how the basic nature of child maltreatment is understood—one that has major implications for the creation and application of definitional schemes. Three of the variables that were assigned epistemological priority by one of the definitional schemes reviewed above are in essence developing systems. The status of the child as a developing system has been clearly recognized for decades (Kessen, 1965). In recent years, the concept of systematic developmental changes during the adult years has taken firm hold in the psychological literature (Baltes and Schaie, 1973; Levinson, 1974; Nesselroade and Reese, 1973) as well as in the popular press (Sheehy, 1976). Even the cultural-historical environment (Bronfenbrenner's "Macrosystem") can be viewed as developing in some fashion, if not as systematically as the child (White, 1976). In addition, as the ecological approach to human development demonstrates, it is fruitful to view the parent-child-environment relationships that constitute acts of maltreatment as developing systems.

Thus, we wish to propose that the basic nature of the phenomenon of child maltreatment be understood as developmental: a developing system of developing systems. This may sound like semantic overkill but we believe it is not. For too long even the most sophisticated interactional theories of child maltreatment have approached the parent, child and environment as if they were static systems (Cicchetti and Rizley, this volume). We contend that fundamental mistakes in creating and applying definitions of child maltreatment are inevitable until the developmental nature of the phenomenon is more fully recognized and accounted for.

The importance of emphasizing the developmental nature of child maltreatment has been most clearly articulated by legal scholars in their efforts to construct legal definitions. And while we will focus on the concept of the child as a developing system and its implications for legal definitions of child maltreatment, we will also argue below that this developmental emphasis is not less important in considering parental or environmental contributions to maltreatment or for clinical or research definitions. The remainder of this paper will be devoted to considering some of the many implications of the developmental orientation for creating and using definitions of child maltreatment.

The Child's Developmental Status. Before the publication by Goldstein, Freud, and Solnit of their work, *Beyond the Best Interests of the Child* (1973) few modern legal scholars considered the developmental stage of the child as a critical characteristic in creating and applying legal definitions of child maltreatment. The few legal debates that did consider a child's age were in other areas of juvenile law and focused on such issues as the age at which a child should be held responsible for certain delinquent or criminal acts. In the 1960s the legal profession as a whole began to turn to social science in general and psychology and psychiatry in particular for guidance on a broad range of issues (standards for competency to stand trial, the social psychology of jury selection, and so on). In part, the recent interest of the law in child development reflects this general trend. In addition, psychology and psychiatry have traditionally found certain legal issues theoretically challenging, for instance, the meaning of criminal insanity (Fingarette, 1972). Some lawyers and psychologists have long considered juvenile and family courts to be virtual field stations for research in developmental psychopathology (Levine and Levine, 1970).

Against the backdrop of this long tradition of mutual interest between law and psychology, the Goldstein, Freud, and Solnit effort marks a qualitative change in construing developmental issues as fundamental to framing certain legal issues appropriately. In attempting to resolve legal dilemmas facing judges and lawyers over child custody decisions in divorce and separation cases, Goldstein and colleagues suggested basic reappraisal of how a child's need for continuity of care and a child's psychological sense of time (both developmental functions) should form the basis for more enlightened legal policies. They argued that young children are vulnerable to the ambiguity and confusion surrounding protracted custody disputes because they experience the length of time required to make the decision as much longer than adults do and because their relationships with their psychological parents are much more threatened by real or potential separations. Therefore, custody decisions should take less time and be final. Psychoanalytically informed developmental psychology, especially the works of Anna Freud herself (1965; 1973) and John Bowlby (1969; 1973) in England on the age-specific effects of separation and loss on child development, presented the scientific foundation for this reappraisal.

Serious critiques of this effort were mounted on a number of fronts. Empirically oriented psychologists, for instance, questioned whether the data on the adverse effects of separation and loss were as solid as Goldstein and others implied (Ellsworth and Levy, 1969). Scholars and practitioners in protective services took Goldstein and colleagues to task for insufficiently distinguishing child custody issues in abuse/neglect cases from custody issues in separation/divorce cases. And social theorists lectured the authors on the more general responsibilities of behavioral science experts in the policy-creation process to cite relevant contradictory data (Katkin, Bullington and Levine, 1974). In fact, Goldstein and colleagues felt sufficiently dissatisfied with the limits of their own work, especially as it related to the issue of coercive state intervention and custody decision making in abuse/neglect cases, that they soon began work on a second volume (Goldstein, Freud, and Solnit, 1978).

Nevertheless, it is fair to say that their first work and the work of young legal scholars under their tutelage (Wald, 1975; 1976) have ushered in a new era of interest in the question of how developmental considerations should influence the creation and application of legal definitions of child maltreatment.

Defining Emotional Damage: A Developmental Approach. If the maltreated child is viewed as a developing system and not simply a static one, a number of issues arise with implications for the definitional problem.

Let us first consider the Juvenile Justice Standards Project proposal to premise all forms of state intervention in child maltreatment cases on specific harms to the child. To construct inclusion and exclusion rules based upon these standards for deciding which potential cases are child maltreatment cases, one must be able to answer such questions as "has this child been seriously harmed?" or "is there a substantial likelihood that this child will imminently be seriously harmed?" The answers to these questions depend on the nature of criteria of harm employed and how the criteria are applied.

Wisely, the Juvenile Justice Standards Project has pointed the legal profession in the direction of requiring that actual harms be specified and documented: as noted above, physical harm must cause disfigurement, impairment of bodily function, or other serious physical injuries; similarly, emotional damage must be evidenced by "severe anxiety, depression or withdrawal, an untoward aggression toward self or others" (Juvenile Justice Standards Project, 1977, p. 55). (These are not the only criteria required to justify coercive state intervention when children are emotionally damaged. Besides specific harm, the children's parents must not be willing to provide treatment for them.)

In the case of physical injury, the specification and documentation of the actual physical harm is relatively straightforward. Broken bones, bruises, welts, burns are frighteningly tangible. Even hidden injuries causing impairment of bodily function like internal organ damage, malnourishment and the like are readily specified and documentable through modern medical technology.

But what if the actual harm to the child is less tangible than physical injury? This complication arises for many forms of maltreatment (for example, parental neglect) but is nowhere more controversial than in the case of emotional mistreatment. The emotional mistreatment of children can often have more serious developmental consequences than physical injuries. In addition, less tangible harms like emotional mistreatment are more frequent as grounds for intervention than more concrete harms like physical injury. Finally, what compels many reports of physical injury is not just the severity of the physical harm but also the implied emotional harm (Giovannoni and Becerra, 1979).

But the specification and reliable documentation of emotional harm is an extremely difficult and complex task. To the extent that emotional harm is a more culturally relative concept that is also harder to specify and document, the danger of using this classification in racially or culturally biased fashion is increased. In addition, voluntary consent to treatment for emotional harm is considered indispensable to the success of treatment. Quality services for the treatment of emotional problems are so scarce that they cannot even meet the demands of those who voluntarily request or consent to treatment. These problems have led some commentators to suggest that emotional mistreatment be abandoned as grounds for justifying coercive state intervention into private family life (Solnit, 1980). This suggestion arises in part because of the confusion between the concepts of "emotional mistreatment" and "emotional damage." The first term refers to parental acts or behaviors, the second term refers to harms to the child. While it is extremely difficult to specify and document what parental acts are emotionally abusive or nelgectful, it may be more possible to specify and document cases of emotional damage (Juvenile Justice Standards Project, 1977, pp. 56–58). In other words, the JJSP focus on harms to the child (not characteristics of the parent or nature of the act of maltreatment) solves many of the problems of those who find "emotional mistreatment" too elusive a concept to form a legal basis for intervention. But a number of serious complications in specifying and documenting harms remain even if "emotional damage" to the child becomes the criterion.

We have referred to the requirement of specific evidence of emotional damage (severe anxiety, depression or withdrawal or untoward aggression toward self or others) to justify intervention as a legal parallel to the operationalism of empirical social or behavioral science research. These terms represent a real improvement over the vague, unspecified criteria for emotional harm previously in use. But we believe that legal scholars and practitioners will discover what developmental psychologists have known for a long time: it is easier to specify in general theoretical fashion an overarching psychological construct that one is interested in over the course of the childhood years (for example, aggression) than it is to operationalize the construct so that it can be used in decision rules about cases. This is so because: first, the expression of the psychological construct by the child, its form and process, varies enormously with developmental stages of the child; second, therefore the methods used to assess or operationalize the construct must be age-appropriate.

Stated another way, in order to use the proposed JJSP standard of emotional damage to create inclusion and exclusion rules to define cases of child maltreatment, one must be able to answer not just the general question "Is this child suffering from emotional damage?" but also the specific question, "Is this child suffering from severe anxiety, depression or withdrawal or untoward aggression toward self or others?" Attempts to answer this question will raise the complication that a depressed toddler presents a very different symptom picture from a depressed preschool child, or that the structure and dynamics of the preschool child's aggression are very different from the structure and dynamics of the school-age child's aggression. Furthermore, severe depression and untoward aggression must be distinguished from moderate and normal aggression because the severe forms of emotional damage can serve to justify coercive state intervention while the moderate forms presumably cannot. Thus, the operational criteria employed by decision makers to include or exclude children as severely depressed, withdrawn, or aggressive should be adjusted to accommodate data on developmental trends.

What is known about trends in the development of these specific forms of emotional damage that could help us operationalize these constructs for use in legal definitions? Let us take the examples of withdrawal, aggression, and depression in turn, briefly discuss some relevant theory and data to illustrate the need to consider their developmental nature, and then clarify their implications for creating and applying definitions of child maltreatment.

Withdrawal. Two important research traditions in developmental psychology have amassed sufficient data on the age-specific nature of social approach and avoidance tendencies in children to merit close attention in our efforts to operationalize the concept of withdrawal.

The first tradition, attachment theory and research, which grew out of the work of John Bowlby in England and Mary Ainsworth in America, is based on an ethological framework. Ainsworth's research on the normal development of attachment relations has documented the changing ways in which infant and mother continually negotiate the dual tasks of maintenance of proximity and exploration of the environment. She has discovered three broad types of attachment relations: secure, anxious/ambivalent and anxious/avoidant (Ainsworth, Blehar, Waters and Wall, 1978). Compared to the securely attached children, anxious/avoidant children interact less harmoniously and less cooperatively with both mothers and peers (Lieberman, 1977; Waters, Wippman and Sroufe, 1979). Especially important to our discussion, the anxious/avoidant infants and toddlers exhibit severe approach/avoidance conflicts including less responsiveness to friendly unfamiliar adults, more negative affect, and less competence in problem-solving situations.

Until the last two years, theory and research on the normal development of infant social relations could only be applied speculatively to issues in the identification and assessment of abused/neglected infants. But the recent work of George and Main (1979) begins the empirical study of social relations of maltreated infants. They have found that physically abused children in a daycare setting remarkably resemble anxious/avoidant children, exhibiting similar patterns of severe approach/avoidance conflicts both with peers and with adults. In addition, Gordon and Jameson (1979) and Egeland and Sroufe (this volume) are beginning to report data actually based on the strange-situation paradigm with failure-to-thrive infants and infants of parents from high risk populations.

Attachment theory and research raises two important issues for definitional schemes of child maltreatment that include withdrawal. First, these findings suggest that at least before the age of two years, withdrawal is best understood as a conflict between two tendencies, not just the expression of one tendency, and includes not just extreme avoidance (commonly thought of as withdrawal) but also lack of effective approach. Second, in Ainsworth's recent essay (1980), she extends the possibility that attachment theory and research can provide the basis for the development of marker instruments to identifying cases of child abuse for intervention. Because of her diagnostic approach to defining child maltreatment, she refers primarily to the potential of DeLozier's work (1979) for developing instruments to assess parental characteristics. Consequently, she misses the equally important point that if harm to the child is the factor on which legal intervention is to be premised, the attachment paradigm and developmental findings based upon it could also become one method of operationalizing the concept of withdrawal in age-appropriate fashion for infants and toddlers.

Attachment research has not yet addressed the social approach/avoidance tendencies of preschool and school-age children (although some longitudinal research that began with attachment relations in infancy is beginning to be conducted into later years; see Arend, Gove and Sroufe, 1979; Egeland and Sroufe, this volume; Sroufe, 1979a). Rather, a second, unrelated research tradition based upon social reinforcement theory has begun to empirically specify the form and process of social approach/avoidance conflicts during these years. Over the past two decades, Zigler and his colleagues have studied the effects of social deprivation on the social and motivational development of preschool and early school-age children (Balla and Zigler, 1975; Harter and Zigler, 1974).

In general, their findings indicate that a history of social deprivation sharply increases the child's need for and responsivity to adult social reinforcement as well as the child's tendency to approach an unfamiliar adult. This need for adult attention may in turn limit the child's freedom to pursue important nonsocial developmental tasks, for instance, those comprising the effectance motive (White, 1959). A second tendency has been identified among some deprived children. Their need for adult attention is at first limited by their tendency to use their first contact with a novel adult to ascertain the rules of the relationship and establish whether the adult is safe. Wariness seems in these children to conflict with their need for adult attention. Thus, the form and process of withdrawal from novel adults during the preschool and school-age years is also best understood as a conflict, but a conflict between the desire for attention and wariness as well as between physical approach and avoidance.

On the basis of this research tradition, it is interesting to speculate whether the increased need for adult attention is associated with a history of social deprivation that child maltreatment practitioners would characterize as neglected and whether increased wariness is related to a social history that would be described as abusive. Research on this issue is presently being conducted by Aber and his colleagues at the Harvard Child Maltreatment Project (Cicchetti and Rizley, this volume). Social deprivation theory and research may prove helpful in operationalizing the concept of withdrawal for the preschool and school-age years.

Certain developmental themes clearly link the findings of attachment research for infants and toddlers and social deprivation research for preschool and school-age children, namely the effects of social histories on children's relations with unfamiliar adults and on children's ability to explore the environment.

But how these themes are played out seems to vary with developmental stages. Certain issues are particularly salient at one age or another (Erikson, 1950; Sander, 1962; Sroufe, 1979b). For instance, the children's relation to their primary caretaker assumes special importance during the first two years of life, whereas children's relation to unfamiliar adults, while theoretically and practically interesting in shedding light on the nature of parent/child relations during the first two years, becomes a more crucial issue in its own right when caretakers outside the immediate family begin to assume major socialization roles, more often between the third and sixth year when children enter group daycare, nursery school, kindergarten, or first grade. Perhaps these differences in the salience of unfamiliar adults to the child explain why abused and anxious/avoidant infants and toddlers appear to be less responsive to unfamiliar adults, whereas socially deprived preschool and school-age children, even the wary children, seem to be more responsive to unfamiliar adults.

Variations in cognitive level of development may also influence the changes in the form and process of withdrawal. For a child operating on a sensori-motor level of intellectual development before the attainment of object permanence, the presence or absence of an adult is more of an all-or-none phenomenon. Thus, withdrawal can carry with it drastically different stakes: if the adult is unfamiliar and unimportant to the child, the child easily denies the adult's existence in the adult's absence; if the adult is an attachment figure of crucial importance to the child, the consequences of withdrawal can be psychic flooding of negative affect. By contrast, the concrete-operational child has grown in cognitive and linguistic abilities to the point where physical withdrawal from an adult does not necessarily entail withdrawal on the symbolic level. The child can comfort himself with fantasies, stories, images, and so on, in a fashion that limits the potential costs of withdrawal. But the child similarly finds it more difficult to deny totally the importance of an adult by simply physically withdrawing. Thus, the profile of costs/benefits of withdrawal systematically changes with developmental stages. Empirical research is clearly needed to begin to describe the specific consequences of an abused/neglected child's level of cognitive development on his social approach and avoidance patterns.

Aggression. Developmental trends in the structure and dynamics of aggressive behavior are more clearly documented than the trends in social approach/avoidance behavior. Shifts in at least four important aspects of aggressive behavior occur sometime from infancy through school-age years.

First, systematic changes occur in the immediate cause of aggressive outbursts (Feshbach, 1970). For instance according to Gardner (1978), infants become aggressive when they are ignored, are in mild physical discomfort, or their movements are restricted. Toddlers, on the other hand, become angry when forced to establish certain routines (for example, bladder control), required to submit to adult authority, or coerced by playmates' demands.

Second, the type of aggressive behavior displayed by a child changes with developmental level. Instrumental aggression, caused by frustration with the physical world and directed toward inanimate objects, is most frequent in the preschool years and usually ends when the child obtains the desired object. Hostile aggression is more dominant during the school-age years, is usually triggered by a threat to the child's self-esteem or the child's perception that he has been intentionally harmed, and is directed at the person who is the source of the threat or harm. Normally, hostile aggression is terminated when the child feels he has reciprocated (Feshbach, 1970; Hartup, 1974).

Third, a developmental trend in the dominant mode of expressing aggressive drives has been documented by Santostefano (1978). During the preschool years, aggression is expressed largely in an action mode. In the early school years, children also employ fantasy as an alternate mode of expression. Finally, language becomes the dominant method of expressing one's anger. In short, "as children gain the capacity to carry out acts in their fantasy life and to express their feelings in words, they become better able to deflect impulses that might physically harm another person and learn to hurt their tormentors instead with psychological weapons" (Gardner, 1978, p. 319). This developmental trend may also account for the observation that physical aggression and tantrums decrease from toddler through the early school-age years (Feshbach, 1970).

Fourth, the child's cognitive understanding of his own aggressive behavior and, most significantly, of aggressive behavior directed toward him changes. For instance, Piaget (1962) has described how a child's moral judgments undergo a change of focus: at first children consider the consequences of acts but eventually base their judgments on the intentions of the actors. Zigler and Child (1973) note that this shift requires a developmental change in logical operations of thought, including increased differentiation of the physical and mental realms. Zigler (1980) has recently noted that it is precisely such developmental shifts in a child's understanding of parental actions that may make the child increasingly vulnerable to emotional mistreatment.

These dramatic shifts in the form and process of aggressive behavior place a premium on a developmental approach to assessing the severity of aggression if it is to be used as a specific criteria for state intervention to protect a child from emotional damage. A developmental approach complicates easy answers to the question, "how severe must the child's aggression be to justify intervention?" One cannot say simply that it depends on whether the target is a person or an object, or whether the act was intentional or accidental, or whether the mode of expression was physical or verbal, since all these dimensions, which may signal increased severity in a static system, are in a state of flux in a developing system.

Depression. The failure of both clinical and experimental psychopathology to consider adequately the stage-specific expression of common underlying problems has limited both theory and research on depression in childhood. In fact, until recently most psychopathologists believed that children could not become depressed because children were not considered in possession of the psychic structures required to become depressed (such as a developed superego) and because children virtually never presented a symptom picture similar to depressed adults (Rie, 1966). This point of view prevailed despite the works of researchers like Spitz and Bowlby documenting children's depressive-like reactions to extreme situations of separation and loss. And while empirical research on childhood depression is still rare, there are signs of growth in theoretical work in childhood depression (Arieti and Bemporad, 1978; French and Berlin, 1979). One of the most important efforts to date is Philips' recent theoretical statement (1979), arguing that depressive symptoms vary with a child's developmental stage. He describes some of the depressive symptoms unique to infancy, including anaclitic depression and failure to thrive. In the preschool years, he views passive aggression and separation anxiety as possible expressions of underlying depression. During the early school-age years, Philips alerts us to school refusal, aggression, learning problems, and hyperactivity as possible symptoms of depression. He concludes that the manifestations of depressive disorders in childhood seem to reflect the developmental capabilities of the child. If severe depression is to remain an important criteria for defining cases of emotional damage, empirical research focused upon a description of stage-specific expressions of depressive symptomatology will be necessary to increase the reliability and validity of the classification.

These manifest expressions of emotional damage—withdrawal, depression, and aggression—are not independent and discrete symptoms. On the contrary, Achenbach (1979) has found that the symptoms of depression and social withdrawal can be combined with other symptoms like somatization to form one major dimension of psychopathological symptoms in childhood. He describes children who score high on this dimension as "internalizers," children whose basic conflicts reside within the self. Similarly, aggressive behaviors can be combined with delinquent-like symptoms (another possible criterion for intervention in the JJSP scheme) to form a second dimension. Children who exhibit a high number of these symptoms are described as "externalizers," children who are in conflict with their social environment. Recently Achenbach (1980) has found it advantageous to establish different norms for preschool (4–6 years) and school-age (6–11 years) boys and girls in devising age-appropriate "child behavior profiles." In short, the criteria justifying state intervention to protect children from emotional harm of mistreatment are intercorrelated, and the precise nature of these intercorrelations, as well as the manifest expressions of the harms themselves, seem to change systematically with developmental stages.

These developmental trends in the manifestation of emotional damage suggest the need to educate legal and clinical decision makers about them so that they can more accurately identify emotionally damaged children. Mistakes of including invalid cases within the classification and excluding valid cases presently occur simply because gatekeepers in protective service systems are so unfamiliar with how emotionally damaged children appear at different stages of development. The data on developmental trends in the form and process of withdrawal, aggression, and depression suggest that without a developmental perspective, the core issue in defining child maltreatment for legal purposes, namely the severity of the type of harm to the child, is extraordinarily difficult to evaluate. The manifest expression of an emotional harm can only be properly evaluted against a stage-related norm. Too much systematic variation in the expression of harm exists to do otherwise.

Two other implications of a developmental perspective on the child for defining child maltreatment occur to us and will be briefly noted here. They both have the greatest implications for case management and research definitions of maltreatment. First, it seems extremely likely that the stimulus value of the child for provoking abusive behaviors from the parent varies systematically with developmental level of the child. For instance, much has been made of the rage some parents feel under some conditions toward helpless, inconsolable infants, especially those with cries of the premature (Frodi and Lamb, 1980). Other parents find toddlers' emerging abilities to locomote and cause a mess more provocative. Feshbach (1980) raises still another stage-related provocation: as children approach the "age of reason," the shift from preoperational to concrete operational thought, they are likely increasingly viewed by parents as beings capable of intentional actions for which they can and should be held responsible. As Feshbach points out from a review of experimental research, a provocative action is more likely to result in an aggressive response if it is seen as the intentional act of a responsible person. Operating within the

JJSP's definitional schema, children's provocation should have no influence on defining child maltreatment, since it focuses exclusively on harms to the child. But to the extent that a clinical or research definition of maltreatment also considers parental characteristics and the nature of the act, an unprovoked action might be more easily defined as abusive than a provoked action.

Second, there are systematic changes with developmental level in children's vulnerabilities to types of maltreatment. We are not invoking a critical-state theory here so much as a vulnerable-period notion. For instance, as described above, severe emotional damage due to separation and loss may be particularly easy to inflict during the child's earliest years. But not all vulnerabilities are based on the assumption that younger children are always most vulnerable. Vulnerability to sexual abuse seems to increase with age straight through to adolescence. And fostering delinquency holds its greatest risk during the early school-age years when social standards are being internalized. The implication of children's shifts in vulnerabilities for defining child maltreatment relates to the distinction between the nature of the act and the harm to the child as the determining factor in defining maltreatment. Clearly an act which may cause harm to a child at one vulnerable stage of development may not at another stage. Are such acts to be included as cases of child maltreatment?

The Parent and the Environment as Developing Systems. Predictive approaches to identifying parents with potential for maltreating their children have been based on profiles of demographic and clinical risk factors developed from analysis in cases of parents who did maltreat their children. By and large, these risk factors have been conceived of as static traits. Examples of demographic risk factors include a single/teenage mother who is the child's primary caretaker and unemployed/financially stressed head of the household. A commonly cited clinical risk factor is age-inappropriate expectations of the child.

For a moment, consider reconceptualizing each of these static traits as manifestations of powerful developmental trends: single parent/teenage mothers as a reflection of the development of adult attachment relationships and social support systems; unemployment/financial stress as related to the development of adult social competence and self-esteem; and age-inappropriate expectations of the child as immature social-cognitive and moral development. Conceived as deviations in development rather than static traits, these risk factors can no longer be used so simply (or dangerously) to identify potentially abusive parents, because the factors themselves are in a state of developmental flux (Cicchetti and Aber, 1980). On the other hand, their predictive and explanatory power as parts of a larger theory of child maltreatment are potentially considerably enhanced.

Viewing the environment as a developing system also has implications for defining child maltreatment. Primarily, it highlights the fact that the cultural context of parent/child relations is also constantly in flux. For instance, shifts in the demography of a culture, especially its population level and the ability of the prevailing technology and political economy to support the population level, have been linked by historically minded psychologists (Bakan, 1971) and anthropologists (Harris, 1979) to shifts in the culture's level of violence to children. They argue that violence to children functions as a form of population control, both directly by eliminating some members of the culture and indirectly by limiting the procreativity of victims. Thus, analysis of the social and economic development of a culture can shed light on the environmental sources of violent parent/child relations (see also Daly and Wilson, this volume).

Changes in a culture's technological and economic capacities to support its population levels are related to both biological and social evolutionary processes. Campbell (1975) offers an intriguing view of the relationship between biological and social evolution and their impact on individual-level behavior. He theorizes that "human urban social complexity has been made possible by social evolution rather than biological evolution" (p. 1115) and that "social evolution has had to counter individual selfish tendencies which biological evolution has continued to select as a result of the genetic competition among the cooperators" (p. 1115). In this context, he urges psychologists and other social scientists to entertain the hypothesis that sociocultural phenomena transmitted across generations (such as organizational structures, customs, beliefs, and — especially important for this discussion — childrearing attitudes and practices) are the products of a social evolutionary process. As such, they possess an inherent "adaptive evolutionary value or an underlying functional truth which social scientists need to understand." (p. 1106). If scholars and practitioners working in the field of child maltreatment heeded Campbell's advice, all cross-generational patterns of childrearing attitudes and practices, including abusive/neglectful attitudes and practices, would be understood in the context of adaptive evolutionary processes.

In summary, demographic and political-economic developments are related to changes in childrearing values that form the normative backdrop against which parental acts and child effects are evaluated. To view the material and value context of child maltreatment as constantly and systematically evolving has perhaps the most profound implication for definitional schemes. It requires us to face the fact that as our culture and society change, our definitions of child maltreatment must change too. In very many senses, the definer's task is a developmental task.

Summary

Analysis of the modern history of efforts to formally define child maltreatment revealed the potential advantages derived from distinguishing among

26

at least three unique and necessary types of definitional schemes for legal and clinical decision making and for research, as well as from assigning epistemological status to parent, act, child, and environment. After these fundamental clarifications in the social and professional aims for which definitions are employed and in the basic elements required for defining maltreatment, this chapter reconceptualized the basic nature of child maltreatment as a developing system of developing systems. The implications of this developmental emphasis, especially in regarding the child as a developing system, on the creation and application of definitional schemes was discussed. The chapter presented a developmental approach to operationalizing the concept of "emotional damage" and explored the impact of this approach on a legal definitional scheme.

References

Aber, J. L. "The Involuntary Child Placement Decision: Solomon's Dilemma Revisited." In G. Gerbner, C. Ross, and E. Zigler (Eds.), *Child Abuse: An Agenda for Action.* New York: Oxford University Press, 1980.

Achenbach, T. M. "The Child Behavior Profile: An Empirically Based System for Assessing Children's Behavioral Problems and Competencies." *International Journal of Mental Health,* 1979, *7*, 24–42.

Achenbach, T. M. "DSM-III in Light of Empirical Research on the Classification of Child Psychopathology." *Journal of the American Academy of Child Psychiatry,* 1980, *19*, 395–412.

Ainsworth, M. D. S. "Attachment and Child Abuse." In G. Gerbner, C. Ross, and E. Zigler (Eds.), *Child Abuse: An Agenda for Action.* New York: Oxford University Press, 1980.

Ainsworth, M. D. S., Blehar, M., Waters, E., and Wall, S. *Patterns of Attachment: A Psychological Study of the Strange Situation.* Hillsdale, N.J.: Erlbaum, 1978.

Alvy, K. T. "Preventing Child Abuse." *American Psychologist,* 1975, *30*(9), 921–928.

Arend, R., Gove, F., and Sroufe, L. A. "Continuity of Individual Adaptation from Infancy to Kindergarten: A Predictive Study of Ego-resiliency and Curiosity in Preschoolers." *Child Development,* 1979, *50*, 950–959.

Arieti, S., and Bemporad, J. *Severe and Mild Depression.* New York: Basic Books, 1978.

Bakan. D. *Slaughter of the Innocents.* San Francisco: Jossey-Bass, 1971.

Balla, D., and Zigler, E. "Preinstitutional Social Deprivation and Responsiveness to Social Reinforcement in Institutionalized, Retarded Individuals: A Six-year Follow-up Study." *American Journal of Mental Deficiency,* 1975, *80*, 228–230.

Baltes, P. B., and Schaie, K. W. "On Life-span Developmental Research Paradigms: Retrospects and Prospects." In P. B. Baltes and K. W. Schaie (Eds.), *Life-span Developmental Psychology: Personality and Socialization.* New York: Academic Press, 1973.

Belsky, J. "Child Maltreatment: An Ecological Integration." *American Psychologist,* 1980, *35*, 320–335.

Bowlby, J. *Attachment and Loss.* Vol. 1: *Attachment.* New York: Basic Books, 1969.

Bowlby, J. *Attachment and Loss.* Vol. 2: *Separation: Anxiety and Anger.* New York: Basic Books, 1973.

Bronfenbrenner, U. "Toward an Experimental Ecology of Human Development." *American Psychologist,* 1977, *32*, 513–531.

Caffey, J. "Multiple Fractures in the Long Bones of Infants Suffering from Chronic Subdural Hematoma." *American Journal of Roentgenology*, 1946, *56*(2), 163–173.

Campbell, D. T. "On the Conflicts Between Biological and Social Evolution and Between Psychology and Moral Tradition." *American Psychologist*, 1975, *30*(12), 1103–1126.

Cicchetti, D., and Aber, J. L. "Abused Children-Abusive Parents: An Overstated Case?" *Harvard Educational Review*, 1980, *50*(2), 244–255.

Cicchetti, D., Taraldson, B., and Egeland, B. "Perspectives in the Treatment and Understanding of Child Abuse." In A. Goldstein (Ed.), *Prescriptions for Child Mental Health and Education.* Elmsford, New York: Pergamon Press, 1978.

DeLozier, P. "An Application of Attachment Theory to the Study of Child Abuse." Unpublished doctoral dissertation, California School of Professional Psychology, 1979.

Ellsworth, P. C., and Levy, R. J. "Legislative Reform of Child Custody Adjudication: An Effort to Rely on Social Science Data in Formulating Legal Policies." *Law and Society Review*, 1969, *4*(2), 167–233.

Erikson, E. H. *Childhood and Society.* New York: Norton, 1950.

Feshbach, S. "Aggression." In P. H. Mussen (Ed.), *Carmichael's Manual of Child Psychology*, Vol. 2. New York: Wiley, 1970.

Feshbach, S. "Child Abuse and the Dynamics of Human Aggression and Violence." In G. Gerbner, C. Ross, and E. Zigler (Eds.), *Child Abuse: An Agenda for Action.* New York: Oxford University Press, 1980.

Fingarette, H. *The Meaning of Criminal Insanity.* Berkeley: University of California Press, 1972.

French, A., and Berlin, I. (Eds.), *Depression in Children and Adolescents.* New York: Human Sciences Press, 1979.

Freud, A. *Normality and Pathology in Childhood.* New York: International Universities Press, 1965.

Freud, A., and Burlingham, D. "Infants Without Families: Reports on the Hampstead Nurseries." In *The Writings of Anna Freud.* Vol. III. New York: International Universities Press, 1973.

Frodi, A. M., and Lamb, M. "Child Abusers' Responses to Infant Smiles and Cries." *Child Development*, 1980, *52*(1), 238–241.

Garbarino, J. "A Preliminary Study of Some Ecological Correlates of Child Abuse: The Impact of Socioeconomic Stress on Mothers." *Child Development*, 1976, *47*(1), 1780–1785.

Garbarino, J., and Crouter, A. "Defining the Community Context for Parent-Child Relations: The Correlates of Child Maltreatment." *Child Development*, 1978, *49*,(3), 604–616.

Gardner, H. *Developmental Psychology.* Boston: Little, Brown, 1978.

Gelles, R. J. "The Social Construction of Child Abuse." *American Journal of Orthopsychiatry*, 1975, *45*(3), 363–371.

Gelles, R. J. "A Profile of Violence toward Children in the United States." In G. Gerbner, C. Ross, and E. Zigler (Eds.), *Child Abuse: An Agenda for Action.* New York: Oxford University Press, 1980.

George, C. E., and Main, M. "Social Interactions of Young Abused Children: Approach, Avoidance, and Aggression." *Child Development*, 1979, *50*, 306–318.

Gil, D. G. *Violence against Children: Physical Abuse in the United States.* Cambridge, Mass.: Harvard University Press, 1970.

Giovannoni, J. M., and Becerra, R. M. *Defining Child Abuse.* New York: Free Press, 1979.

Goldstein, J., Freud, A., and Solnit, A. *Beyond the Best Interests of the Child.* New York: Free Press, 1973.

Goldstein, J., Freud, A., and Solnit, A. *Before the Best Interests of the Child.* New York: Free Press, 1978.

Gordon, A., and Jameson, J. "Infant-Mother Attachment in Patients with Nonorganic Failure to Thrive Syndrome." *Journal of the American Academy of Child Psychiatry,* 1979, *18,* 251-259.

Harris, M. *Cultural Materialism: The Struggle for a Science of Culture.* New York: Random House, 1979.

Harter, S., and Zigler, E. "The Assessment of Effectance Motivation in Normal and Retarded Children." *Developmental Psychology,* 1974, *10,* 169-180.

Hartup, W. W. "Aggression in Childhood: Developmental Perspectives." *American Psychologist,* 1974, *29,* 336-341.

Juvenile Justice Standards Project. *Standards Relating to Abuse and Neglect.* Cambridge, Mass.: Ballinger, 1977.

Katkin, D., Bullington, B., and Levine, M. "Above and Beyond the Best Interests of the Child: An Inquiry into the Relationship Between Social Science and Social Action." *Law and Society Review,* 1974, *8,* 669-687.

Kempe, C. H., Silverman, F., Steele, B., Droegemueller, W., and Silver, H. "The Battered Child Syndrome." *Journal of the American Medical Association,* 1962, *181*(1), 17-24.

Kessen, W. *The Child.* New York: Wiley, 1965.

Levine, M., and Levine, A. *Social History of the Helping Services.* New York: Appleton-Century-Crofts, 1970.

Levinson, D. *The Psychological Development of Men in Early Adulthood and the Mid-life Transition.* Minneapolis: The University of Minnesota Press, 1974.

Lieberman, A. F. "Preschooler's Competence with a Peer: Relations with Attachment and Peer Experience." *Child Development,* 1977, *48*(4), 1277-1287.

Meehl, P. E. "Theoretical Risks and Tabular Asterisks: Sir Karl, Sir Ronald, and the Slow Progress of Soft Psychology." *Journal of Consulting and Clinical Psychology,* 1978, *46*(4), 806-834.

Nesselroade, J. R., and Reese, H. W. *Life-span Developmental Psychology — Methodological Issues.* New York: Academic Press, 1973.

Pfohl, S. "The 'Discovery' of Child Abuse." *Social Problems,* 1977, *24,*(3), 310-323.

Philips, I. "Childhood Depression: Interpersonal Interactions and Depressive Phenomena." *American Journal of Psychiatry,* 1979, *136*(48), 511-515.

Piaget, J. *The Moral Judgment of the Child.* New York: Collier, 1962.

Popper, K. R. *The Logic of Scientific Discovery.* New York: Basic Books, 1959.

Radbill, S. X. "A History of Child Abuse and Infanticide." In R. E. Helfer and C. H. Kempe (Eds.), *The Battered Child.* Chicago: University of Chicago Press, 1974.

Rie, H. E. "Depression in Childhood: A Survey of Some Pertinent Contributions." *Journal of the American Academy of Child Psychiatry,* 1966, *5,* 653-685.

Ross, C. J. "The Lessons of the Past: Defining and Controlling Child Abuse in the United States." In G. Gerbner, C. Ross, and E. Zigler (Eds.), *Child Abuse: An Agenda for Action.* New York: Oxford University Press, 1980.

Ross, C., Aber, L., Alexander, K., Heller, K., Nelson, K., and Phillips-DeMott, D. Conference recommendations on child abuse, November 20-21, 1978, Philadelphia, Pa. Available from ERIC Clearinghouse.

Ross, C., and Zigler, E. "An Agenda for Action." In G. Gerbner, C. Ross, and E. Zigler (Eds.), *Child Abuse: An Agenda for Action.* New York: Oxford University Press, 1980.

Sander, L. "Issues in Early Mother-Child Interaction." *Journal of the American Academy of Child Psychiatry,* 1962, *1,* 141-166.

Santostefano, S. *A Biodevelopmental Approach to Clinical Child Psychology.* New York: Wiley, 1978.

Sheehy, G. *Passages: Predictable Crises of Adult Life.* New York: Dutton, 1976.

Solnit, A. "Too Much Reporting, Too Little Service: Roots and Prevention of Child Abuse." In G. Gerbner, C. Ross, and E. Zigler (Eds.), *Child Abuse: An Agenda for Action.* New York: Oxford University Press, 1980.

Sroufe, L. A. "Socioemotional Development." In J. Osofsky (Ed.), *Handbook of Infant Development.* New York: Wiley, 1979a.

Sroufe, L. A. "The Coherence of Individual Development: Early Care, Attachment, and Subsequent Developmental Issues." *American Psychologist,* 1979b, *34*(10), 834–841.

Wald, M. "State Intervention on Behalf of 'Neglected' Children: A Search for Realistic Standards." *Stanford Law Review,* 1975, *27*(4), 985–1040.

Wald, M. "State Intervention on Behalf of 'Neglected' Children: Standards for Removal of Children from their Homes, Monitoring the Status of Children in Foster Care, and Termination of Parental Rights." *Stanford Law Review,* 1976, *28,* 623–707.

Waters, E., Wippman, J., and Sroufe, L. A. "Attachment, Positive Affect, and Competence in the Peer Group: Two Studies in Construct Validation." *Child Development,* 1979, *50,* 821–829.

White, R. "Motivation Reconsidered: The Concept of Competence." *Psychological Review,* 1959, *66,* 217–233.

White, S. "Developmental Psychology and Vico's Concept of Universal History." *Social Research,* 1976, *43*(4), 659–571.

Zigler, E. "Controlling Child Abuse: Do We Have the Knowledge and/or the Will?" In G. Gerbner, C. Ross and E. Zigler (Eds.), *Child Abuse: An Agenda for Action.* New York: Oxford University Press, 1980.

Zigler, E., and Child, I. (Eds.) *Socialization and Personality Development.* Reading, Mass.: Addison Wesley, 1973.

Zigler, E., and Phillips, L. "Psychiatric Diagnosis: A Critique." *Journal of Abnormal and Social Psychology,* 1961, *63*(3), 607–618.

J. Lawrence Aber, III, is a predoctoral research fellow at the Bush Center for Child Development and Social P licy, Yale University; clinical fellow in psychology, Beth Israel Hospital, Harvard Medical School; and associate director of the Harvard Child Maltreatment Project, Department of Psychology and Social Relations, Harvard University.

Edward Zigler is Sterling Professor of psychology and director of the Bush Center for Child Development and Social Policy, Yale University.

Research methods and inferential techniques must acknowledge the complexity and heterogeneity of child maltreatment. Empirical investigation of child maltreatment must be guided by sophisticated concepts of development, personality, psychopathology, and family and social systems theory.

Developmental Perspectives on the Etiology, Intergenerational Transmission, and Sequelae of Child Maltreatment

Dante Cicchetti
Ross Rizley

Despite greatly increased public concern, funding, and scientific efforts directed toward child maltreatment during the past decade, we are still far from achieving an adequate understanding of this important problem. Even though heightened interest has been paid to maltreatment phenomena in this era of child advocacy and social policy, we possess only limited information about a number of issues that are central to the formulation of a truly integrative theory of the origins, intergenerational transmission, and sequelae of child maltreatment.

The order of authors' names was decided by a flip of a coin. Both contributed equally to the content and preparation of this chapter. We wish to thank Cecelia Sudia of the National Center on Child Abuse and Neglect, and J. Lawrence Aber and Vicki Carlson-Luden of the Harvard Child Maltreatment Project for their encouragement and many invaluable suggestions. We also wish to thank the officials and especially the social workers of the Massachusetts Department of Social Services and their

We do not yet have an adequate taxonomic system for conceptualizing and reliably differentiating among the different manifestations of maltreatment within the spectrum of maltreatment phenomena (Rizley and Cicchetti, 1980a, c). Despite several promising theoretical conceptions (Belsky, 1980; Cicchetti, Taraldson, and Egeland, 1978; Garbarino, 1977; Parke and Collemer, 1975), we know very little about the antecedent conditions of the different forms of child maltreatment. The limited information that does exist regarding the risk factors that may affect the likelihood of maltreatment is based primarily on a handful of demographic or epidemiologic studies (see, for example, Garbarino, 1976; Garbarino and Crouter, 1978; Gelles, 1978; Gil, 1970; Nagi, 1977). The specific mechanisms and processes by which risk factors lead to an incident of child abuse or neglect have been paid scanty attention until recently. Factors such as stress, social isolation, and a lack of social support systems have been implicated in the etiology of child maltreatment. However, it is now necessary to go beyond correlative models and to begin investigating the specific causal mechanisms by which these factors exert their impact. Not all parents exposed to these risk factors maltreat their children. The mechanisms that intervene between these factors and child maltreatment must be mapped out in far greater detail. An ecological framework (Belsky, 1980; Bronfenbrenner, 1977, 1979; Herrenkohl and Herrenkohl, this volume), which we endorse, sets the stage for an understanding of maltreatment phenomena. However, it provides us only with an elementary, molar language system and structure for comprehending the etiology and sequelae of child maltreatment. We are rapidly approaching the point where it will be necessary for us to go beyond this first level of analysis. More attention must be directed to the specific intervening causal processes. Bruner, Oliver, and Greenfield put forward a similar thesis: "A child does not perform a certain action a certain way at a certain age *because* the culture he lives in exhibits that pattern . . . . What is needed for a psychological explanation is a psychological theory. *How* does a culture in which a child lives affect his way of looking at the world?" (1966, pp. 2–3). We have almost no information concerning the transmission processes by which child maltreatment is passed from one generation to the next, nor do we understand much about the mechanisms that lead to a break in the transmission pattern (Cicchetti and Aber, 1980; Cicchetti and Rizley, 1978; Hunter and Kilstrom, 1979). Moreover, one of the most basic issues,

predecessors at the Massachusetts Department of Public Welfare for their dedicated effort in serving maltreated children and families and their commitment to making this university/government collaboration work. Finally, we are grateful to William Damon for his guidance and assistance in the preparation of this special edition of *New Directions*. The Harvard Child Maltreatment Project described in this paper is supported by Grant No. 90–C–1929 from the National Center on Child Abuse and Neglect, Administration for Children, Youth and Families, Office of Human Development.

documenting the impact that maltreatment has upon the cognitive, socio-emotional, and linguistic development of the child, has only begun to be studied systematically (Elmer, 1977; Kent, 1976; Martin, 1976). Almost no attention has been directed towards the sequelae of maltreatment in terms of its effects upon the socioemotional competence of the child, although its significance in terms of later adaptation is unquestionable (Cicchetti and Sroufe, 1978; Egeland and Sroufe, this volume; Gaensbauer and Sands, 1979; George and Main, 1979; Gordon and Jameson, 1979; Kinard, 1980; Martin, 1976; Reidy, 1977; Sroufe, 1979a, 1979b). What little information exists on the psychological effects of maltreatment on the child primarily concerns cognitive impairments, measured largely in terms of "product" variables such as psychometric tests. The researcher's focus on achievement rather than on processes (Werner, 1937) can lead to the incorrect conclusion that the null hypothesis is true and that maltreatment *per se* has no deleterious effects upon a child's development (see Elmer, 1977). Similarly, the use of age-inappropriate measures or developmentally unsound constructs will only obscure true between- and within-group differences. We have only begun to appreciate the fact that different *types* of maltreatment may have different effects upon a child's development (see Egeland and Sroufe, this volume; Rizley and Cicchetti, 1980a,b). Little is known about the specific developmental systems that are most at risk at differing ages, or about the interaction between type of maltreatment, age of maltreated child, and systems at risk. It is essential that researchers clearly define subgroups of maltreatment within the context of a broader continuum of caretaking casualty (Sameroff and Chandler, 1975). Additionally, the impact of a history of abuse or neglect upon life span development—not just development over a period of a few years—has yet to be addressed through empirical investigation.

When one considers the historically close alignment with the medical profession (see Aber and Zigler, this volume; Radbill, 1968; Ross, 1980), it is not surprising to learn that research on child maltreatment has been dominated by a clinical psychopathological model. Hence, the vast majority of research studies conducted in this area have focused on the personality characteristics of the maltreating parent. The myopic focus upon parental psychopathology as the only cause of child maltreatment has persisted despite growing theoretical and empirical evidence that child maltreatment is the product of a multiplicity of factors—not merely an effect of a single causal factor operating in isolation (Rizley and Cicchetti, 1980a). States differently, there are *multiple* sufficient conditions for the occurrence of child maltreament (Belsky, 1980; Cicchetti, Taraldson, and Egeland, 1978; Gelles, 1973; Herrenkohl and Herrenkohl, this volume; Parke and Collmer, 1975). Moreover, most investigations of parental personality characteristics or parental psychopathology have utilized measures or diagnostic schemes of limited reliability and validity (see, for example, Fiske, 1974; Mischel, 1968). Thus, after scores of studies of parents who maltreat their children, we actually know very little about the potential causal role of psychopathology and personality attributes, nor do we understand the relationship between these variables and the specific type of maltreatment which occurs.

Finally, we have little scientific data bearing on the issue of the efficacy of differing therapeutic interventions (Cicchetti, Taraldson, and Egeland, 1978). Little is known about the interaction between type of maltreatment and treatment response (Rizley and Cicchetti, 1980a,b). In addition, while several prescriptions have been suggested to eradicate the conditions associated with child maltreatment (Gil, 1970; Zigler, 1976), there are few substantive empirical findings on which to base social policies addressing the problem (Light, 1973). If we are to unravel the complex problem of child maltreatment, this paucity of critical information must be remedied.

There are systematic reasons why our knowledge of child maltreatment is rudimentary. One important factor is that it is difficult to study the phenomena of child maltreatment using traditional research paradigms and strategies (Starr, Ceresnie, and Rossi, 1976). An even more basic problem is the difficulty of obtaining an adequate number of representative families to study. Even with an appropriate sample, collecting and obtaining the sensitive information necessary to describe the types of maltreatment which have occurred is problematic. There is no reliable, valid, accepted nosology for describing and classifying the phenomena subsumed under the rubric of child maltreatment, which exacerbates the formidable problems of scientific communication (Rizley and Cicchetti, 1980c). Even when an investigator is fortunate enough to collect reliable information on a sufficiently large and representative cohort, it is difficult to separate the causes of maltreatment from its effects and the multiple consequences of having been identified as a child maltreater. Disentangling the complex causal pathways demands the most sophisticated statistical and research techniques. Moreover, it is clear that to go beyond mere description to an understanding of causes, prospective longitudinal studies are necessary. They are, however, time consuming and expensive and therefore rare (Altemeier, 1978; Egeland and Brunnquell, 1979; Egeland and Sroufe, this volume; Hunter, Kilstrom, Kraybill, and Loda, 1978; O'Connor and others, 1979).

In summary, we think that the limitations in our knowledge in the area of child maltreatment have much to do with research difficulties, and little to do with the intelligence, skill, or motivation of researchers working in this area. The empirical study of child maltreatment is a perplexing scientific problem for which we have no ready answers or simple solutions. However, given the significant scientific and policy issues raised by research in child maltreatment, we must characterize the phenomenon in a way commensurate with its true complexity. Even if they acknowledge the gravity and pervasiveness of maltreatment phenomena (Gelles, 1978, 1980; Gil, 1970; Light, 1973; Nagi, 1977), if researchers present simplistic conceptualizations of its causes and consequences, the importance of such phenomena may be inaccurately dismissed.

We intend in this chapter to outline some of the issues and complexities that have shaped our conception of and approach to the phenomena of child maltreatment and to describe an ongoing, longitudinal research study that we have initiated, investigating the etiology, sequelae, and transmission of child maltreatment.

Heterogeneity of Child Maltreatment

A fundamental difficulty in the study of child maltreatment is that the range of phenomena covered by the term is enormously varied. Child maltreatment is a heterogeneous problem. There are three primary types of heterogeneity with which we must be concerned (Rizley and Cicchetti, 1980a): in symptom pattern or type of maltreatment, in etiology, and in response to treatment. The first type acknowledges the fact that a spectrum of different problems are subsumed under the term of child maltreatment. The second acknowledges that different etiologies or causal networks exist, giving rise to the spectrum of different types of maltreatment. The third type of heterogeneity underscores the observation that there is wide variation in response to treatment interventions among families where there has been maltreatment (Cicchetti, Taraldson, and Egeland, 1978; Kempe and Helfer, 1972; Kempe and Kempe, 1978). The failure to attend to these three sources of heterogeneity has contributed to our less than complete understanding of this important problem.

The most obvious type of heterogeneity is revealed by the different manifestations of child maltreatment—that is, the manifold expressions or symptoms of maltreatment. The array of problems for which parents are legally identified as having maltreated their offspring cannot be grouped together if we wish to find meaningful relationships between causal factors and type of maltreatment, or between treatment response and type of maltreatment. In scientific analyses, the spectrum of problems casually referred to by the terms *child abuse* and *neglect* must be covered by an explicit nosology of maltreatment. As Giovannoni and Becerra's (1979) seminal work so vividly illustrates, it makes little sense to indiscriminantly group together disparate categories. Without clearer definitions, Giovannoni and Becerra fear that some children who require protection will go undetected and other children who are not maltreated will be mislabeled and subjected to unnecessary treatment and intervention. Both types of children, undetected and mislabeled, would benefit from clearer definitions (see also Aber and Zigler, this volume).

Another important rationale for attending to the issue of heterogeneity is that different types of maltreatment may have vastly different effects on the maltreated child and on the maltreating adults and other family members (see Egeland and Sroufe, this volume). For example, we might ask whether acts of omission that harm the child (for example, gross neglect) have as devastating effects upon development as do acts of commission (such as physical abuse or emotional beratement). Nonetheless, research reports often fail adequately to describe types of maltreatment, instead labeling a varied group of families as "child abuse" families. Grouping together all families who have maltreated their children can only lead to confusion and obscure very real differences in etiology, sequelae, cross-generational transmission patterns, and treatment response for different types of maltreatment (Rizley and Cicchetti, 1980a). Researchers should specify the inclusion and exclusion criteria characterizing their respective maltreatment samples (Rizley and Cicchetti, 1980c).

There are numerous reasons why few researchers or theorists differentiate among different types of maltreatment. One is a practical limitation — the information necessary to classify or type the maltreatment is highly sensitive and difficult to obtain. Records are often inadequate sources because record keepers have themselves failed to make the pertinent observations or to record the information necessary for describing different types of maltreatment. Also, it is difficult enough to obtain a sample to study without adding the requirement that the researcher specify precisely what type or types of maltreatment occurred in each case. However, these very practical difficulties in no way obviate the need to obtain careful information about type of maltreatment. At the very least, it is incumbent on the researcher to perform separate analyses of families with grossly different patterns of maltreatment (see Egeland and Sroufe, this volume; Herrenkohl and Herrenkohl, this volume).

An additional reason why some fail to address the issue of type heterogeneity stems from the implicit or explicit assumption, that different types of maltreatment do not exist and that any classification or nosology represents a rather futile effort to divide what is in reality a continuum into discrete categories. The point to be made in this regard is that we can only discover whether or not it is important to worry about type of maltreatment by examining the issue empirically. Failure to attend to this major source of heterogeneity runs the very real risk of ignoring a source of variation that is crucial to an appreciation of the differing etiologies, sequelae, intergenerational transmission patterns, and treatment responses of different types of maltreatment. We suggest that researchers attend carefully to this issue and seek practical, reasonable ways to gather the information necessary to classify or type maltreatment and to assess the utility and validity of these classification schemes.

The practical difficulty of obtaining the kinds of information necessary to "type" maltreatment deserves research attention of its own. Perhaps we can learn a valuable lesson from research in the area of psychopathology. Reliability in the diagnosis of mental disorders for research purposes has been greatly improved by two advances: the establishment of more operational, explicit, and hence reliable criteria for each "type" of mental disorder; and the development of standardized, structured diagnostic interviews. The first improvement reduces the criterion or nosological variance in diagnosis, the second greatly reduces the diagnostician variance—variance due to different diagnosticians, who may have different interviewing styles, different assumptions about signs and symptoms of disorders, and so on. Research on child maltreatment would greatly benefit from the development of similar research instruments, such as a set of more reliable, explicit, and operational criteria for different types of maltreatment analogous to the Research Diagnostic Criteria (RDC) (Spitzer, Endicott, and Robins, 1978a,b) in psychopathology and developing a semi-structured interview modelled after the Schedule of Affective Disorders and Schizophrenia (SADS) (Spitzer and Endicott, 1978a,b) and the Diagnostic Interview Schedule (DIS) (Robins, Helzer, Croughan and Spitzer, 1979) to obtain the information necessary for typing maltreatment. The difficulties and problems associated with this enterprise have been discussed elsewhere (Rizley and Cicchetti, 1980c). We are currently developing preliminary versions of these instruments as part of our longitudinal study of child maltreatment at Harvard University. The development of a structured, sensitive, flexible instrument useful to researchers investigating all types of maltreatment would have the advantage of making more standardized and uniform the interview used to diagnose the particular form or forms of maltreatment. Similarly, establishment of a set of working or operational criteria would have the useful effect of increasing the precision in the definition and description of different types of maltreatment. Clarity of language and communication will be improved if a set of theoretically neutral, but explicit and precise categories can be described operationally and a standardized set of interview and assessment procedures developed. Progress in our understanding awaits, in part, development of research methods and tools sensitive to the problem of heterogeneity and to the problem of different information bases.

Heterogeneity in Developmental Sequelae

Although the seriousness of the immediate problems that result from child maltreatment is clear (see, for example, Kempe and Kempe, 1978; Martin, 1976), only a very few studies have attempted to look at the long-range consequences of child abuse and neglect (see, for example, Egeland and Sroufe, this volume; Elmer, 1977; Herrenkohl and Herrenkohl, this volume; Kent, 1976; Martin and Beezeley, 1977; Terr, 1970). Despite the varying degree of substantive evidence, existing data converge on the fact that maltreated children are adversely affected in a multitude of ways. While the occurrence of death and significant intellectual and neuromuscular anomalies is well documented, the more subtle effects of maltreatment on the child's socioemotional development have been more often the subject of speculation, rather than of empirical study. While investigators have focused primarily on identifying the maltreated child and on pursuing legal and social intervention, more effort should be directed towards establishing developmentally appropriate treatment procedures to alleviate the physical and socioemotional impairments suffered by the child (Cicchetti, Taraldson, and Egeland, 1978; Goldstein, Freud, and Solnit, 1973, 1979; Solnit, 1980; Wald, 1976).

Maltreated children exhibit a wide variety of developmental disabilities, although there is no specific single pattern that could be described as the profile of abuse or neglect (see Egeland and Sroufe, this volume; Herrenkohl and Herrenkohl, this volume). Indeed, it would be surprising were any specific pattern to emerge. Children of different ages, at different developmental stages, from diverse environments, and with differing experiences, who are exposed to vastly different forms of maltreatment, are likely to manifest vulnerabilities and disabilities in a wide variety of specific, age-appropriate ways. Part of the problem in providing maltreated children with timed, guided interventions is to identify the specific vulnerabilities, developmental disabilities or competencies they exhibit and to plan individualized treatments focused on amelioration or remediation of these disabilities. It is impossible to develop cogent, sophisticated diagnostic and treatment plans without a developmental model that tells us where to look for the vulnerabilities. A developmentally sound theoretical model is needed to point us to the processes or systems at highest risk for contributing to vulnerability at each given developmental level. Once we have identified which processes or systems are important for children of a given age grouping, we can identify in any given case of child abuse or neglect the developmental problems involved and design a remedial treatment to target specifically on those issues (see, for example, Furman, Rahe, and Hartup, 1979). Additionally, it should be emphasized that this strategy also lends itself to coordination of the treatment of the parent with that of the child. For example, the parent can be trained to deal more adaptively and effectively with the child's specific problems and difficulties, thereby reducing the probability of future maltreatment. New coping and interactional skills can be built on the firm foundation offered by a developmental assessment of the child's specific problems (Cicchetti and Aber, 1980).

The many important gaps in our knowledge about child maltreatment present impediments to conceptual, empirical, and prescriptive advancements in this area. As Zigler states:

Given the embryonic state of research knowledge in the child abuse area, it is not surprising to discover the area more replete with myths than with well-validated facts. The danger . . . is that when the emphasis is on social action . . . these myths will become the guide to action since they are all that are available to inform social policy and/or intervention efforts (1976, p. 17).

Problems of Inference

Another serious problem confronting researchers in this area is the problem of choosing appropriate control or comparison groups. The literature in the area of child maltreatment is characterized by inadequate and biased sampling, confounding variables, illegitimate inferences, and sweeping generalizations. To determine unambiguously whether a given factor is a cause, in the sense that it increases the probability of child maltreatment, or to assert that a given developmental pattern is the result of maltreatment *per se,* rather than, say, social class or poor quality parenting, it is essential to utilize comparison groups to control for factors unrelated to child maltreatment that may have impact on the dependent measures. A further complication is that the majority of studies in the area have been conducted without attention to even the most elementary principles of experimental design, such as the use of any control groups.

There are at least two different kinds of issues involved in the control/ comparison group question — some practical and some theoretical. The practical issues are most basic — how can one obtain control groups that share many of the demographic and ecological features of the maltreatment group but have no maltreated children? How can one detect maltreatment in the comparison population if it exists? There is a logistic problem here, too — the sheer numbers of comparison subjects needed to control for even a few variables that are important risk factors in child maltreatment. These practical issues dovetail with a more theoretical issue — for what factors do we want to control, or along what dimensions should we compare or match? We must also beware of the matching fallacy — namely, that controlling for every conceivable variable may obscure actual group differences. One needs an adequate theory to guide one to the appropriate comparison groups and measures to employ. While very few researchers have chosen comparison groups on more theoretical grounds (see, for example, Egeland and Sroufe, this volume; Herrenkohl and Herrenkohl, this volume), the vast majority have utilized comparison samples based solely on convenience (see Spinetta and Rigler, 1972).

The type of comparison groups chosen depends on which research questions one is posing. If an investigator's interest is in etiology, then one should sample from comparison groups sharing some but not all hypothesized etiological factors. If one's interest lies in the issue of the developmental sequelae of maltreatment, then one should sample from children and families sharing some but not all of the factors characterizing childrearing practices of parents who maltreat their children. Finally, if one's interest is in the intergenerational transmission issue, then one should choose groups differing on factors important to this dimension.

Another serious methodological shortcoming characterizing the field of child maltreatment is that practically all of the research in child abuse is *ex post facto* and is fraught with all of the flaws that accompany the retrospective research method (see Meehl, 1970; Yarrow, Campbell, and Burton, 1970). Retrospection introduces systematic biases through a variety of nonrandom effects, including: (1) the distorting role of the time interval between incident and report, (2) the influence of contemporary adaptation on recall of past adjustment, and (3) the operation of effects such as current conceptions of what mental health entails (for example, how maltreating parents are conceptualized by society). Furthermore, the use of retrospective research techniques makes it difficult to disentangle characteristics that were present before a maltreatment incident from those that occurred as a result of it. An example of how retrospective research can lead to an inaccurate and simplistic notion of the etiology of child maltreatment is found in the "intergenerational transmission hypothesis." That is, that parents who maltreat their children were themselves maltreated in their childhood and that the children they maltreat are likewise destined to become maltreating parents (see, for example, Spinetta and Rigler, 1972). While some maltreaters have undoubtedly been maltreated, the extent of this occurrence has not been confirmed empirically. Moreover, to imply that all maltreated children will become child maltreaters would result not only in an exorbitant number of false positives but would also create much unnecessary anxiety in prospective parents who were maltreated. Retrospective research could only show what percent of maltreaters were themselves maltreated. It does not enable us to know what percent of children who were maltreated will ultimately maltreat their own children. To suggest that a present problem is caused directly by an event known only through an historical account — and to do so despite the presence of many other factors — only obfuscates the scientific effort to unravel the etiology of this complex problem.

Unfortunately, retrospective inferences also pose problems for the implementation of treatment programs. Empirical attempts to verify the etiology and sequelae of child maltreatment are sorely needed as a basis for the development of effective treatment methods. Therapists who feel that research veridicality is an essential ingredient for prescription are understandably reluctant to implement programs based on nothing more than subjective hypotheses and evaluations. Clearly, we will need many more theoretically based controlled prospective studies before questions of etiology, sequelae, transmission patterns, and treatment response can be answered adequately.

A final inferential problem is that few researchers use adequate statistical techniques for interpreting the complexities inherent in research on child maltreatment, primarily because of the need to explain changes in a variety of transacting systems across time—parent, child, environment, and their mutual influence upon each other. It is now clear that single variables account for relatively small percentages of the variance in most investigations of maltreatment (Herrenkohl and Herrenkohl, this volume). While correlational data or multivariate analyses may provide some indication of relationships, they seldom address the more pressing question of causality. Cross-lag correlation and path analysis coupled with longitudinal designs offer the greatest promise for illuminating the etiology and sequelae of child maltreatment. Within the domain of developmental psychology, path analysis has been increasingly employed in attempts to unravel complex causal linkages. Relationships existing between two variables at different times may result from a multitude of different causal pathways. Path analysis uses regression analyses to choose between these competing causal possibilities. Complex causal networks such as those almost certainly involved in the etiology, transmission, and sequelae of child maltreatment require commensurately complex statistical analyses. Such sophisticated statistical models have yet to be applied to the data from longitudinal studies of child maltreatment.

While we have underscored the fact that research in the field of child maltreatment demands the utmost methodological and conceptual rigor, we do not feel pessimistic about the possibility of meeting these challenges. The development of a firm knowledge base should be given high priority, both by researchers and governmental agencies. Until we buttress our theories and treatment strategies with solid empirical evidence, the myths in our knowledge of child maltreatment that Zigler (1976) eloquently addressed will persist and our attempts to help these children and their families will not be effective.

The Harvard Child Maltreatment Project

In the fall of 1979, we initiated a three-year longitudinal investigation of the etiology, transmission and sequelae of child maltreatment (Cicchetti and Rizley, 1978). Our guiding assumption was that child maltreatment is a complex, heterogeneous phenomenon, with a wide variety of different manifestations, etiologies, and developmental sequelae (Rizley and Cicchetti, 1980a). The scientific perspective with which we approached the problem can best be described as empirical and broad based, drawing on the best theories and measurement techniques from a variety of disciplines—developmental psychology and psychopathology, descriptive and experimental psychopathology, sociology, epidemiology, applied behavioral analysis, and personality assessment.

Our first and most fundamental decision was to study the spectrum of maltreatment phenomena with the explicit goal of developing and validating a "nosology" of child maltreatment (Rizley and Cicchetti, 1980b,c). Hence, we posed the following question:

1. Are There Different Types of Child Maltreatment that Can Be Reliably Differentiated? Our first step was to develop a structured, sensitive, reliable, interview-based measure to define and identify different types of maltreatment (Cicchetti, Rizley, Aber, and Carlson-Luden, 1980). We modelled our interview on the well-known psychiatric interviews developed at the National Institute of Mental Health—the DIS and the SADS. Our goal is to develop a reliable "diagnostic" measure of child maltreatment that will prove useful in developing standardized data bases for defining types of child maltreatment (Rizley and Cicchetti, 1980c). The concurrent development of a set of explicit operational criteria, modeled after the RDC criteria in psychopathology, for the "diagnosis" of different types of maltreatment will greatly increase communication and facilitate research and comparison of results in this area (Rizley and Cicchetti, 1980c).

Given a reliable nosological scheme for child maltreatment, the next issue involves its validity. Do the different types of maltreatment postulated have different consequences, antecedents, treatment responses or transmission patterns? If so, it will be crucial to attend to type of maltreatment in future investigations (Rizley and Cicchetti, 1980b).

Our strategy to validate our developing nosology of maltreatment involves five additional project questions:

2. Do Different Types of Child Maltreatment Have Different Etiologies? While we assume that there are multiple pathways leading to a maltreatment episode, if we can demonstrate that different types in the maltreatment spectrum have identifiably different patterns of risk factors, this would be one means of validating our classificatory scheme.

3. Do Different Types of Child Maltreatment Have Differential Effects on the Development of the Children and upon the Family's Functioning? It is likely that the specific developmental impact of maltreatment experienced by a child or a family will be closely related to the type of maltreatment that has occurred (see, for example, Egeland and Sroufe, this volume). If this can be demonstrated, it will strengthen the confidence we have in the validity of our classification system.

4. Do Different Types of Maltreatment Have Different Patterns of Cross-Generational Transmission? As we have stated, transmission of maltreatment across generations is a common, but by no means an inevitable, consequence of having been maltreated. Do different types of maltreatment leave the maltreated child with differing patterns of risk either to increase the likelihood of or to buffer against the possibility of future maltreatment of his or her own children?

Again, if we can document that there are differential risk patterns of intergenerational transmission for different types of maltreatment, then this would further demonstrate the importance of classifying maltreatment phenomena according to their subtype in the spectrum of child maltreatment.

The approach we have adopted in examining the etiology and transmission issues focuses on the concept of risk factors. We have classified risk factors into two broad categories — *potentiating factors,* which increase the probability of maltreatment, and *compensatory factors,* which decrease the risk of maltreatment. Under each category we distinguish two subgroupings — transient, fluctuating, "state" factors, and more permanent, enduring conditions or attributes. Our scheme for classifying risk factors is shown in Table 1.

Vulnerability factors. Included here are all relatively enduring and long-acting factors, conditions, or attributes that potentiate or increase the risk of maltreatment and its transmission across generations. Vulnerability factors may be biological in nature (for example, a child with a difficult temperament, physical or behavioral anomalies that make childrearing unrewarding or difficult, and so on); historical (for example, a history of being maltreated as a child); psychological (for example, personality attributes such as poor frustration tolerance, psychopathology, or high trait levels of aggression and anger) sociological/cultural (for example, culturally determined childrearing and disciplinary practices); or situational (for example, chronic conditions such as poverty, poor employment opportunities, poor physical environment, poor parenting skills, and so on). They may involve parental, child, or even environmental characteristics.

Table 1. Risk Factors for Child Maltreatment

	Impact on Probability of Maltreatment	
Temporal Dimension	*Potentiating Factors*	*Compensatory Factors*
Enduring Factors	*Vulnerability Factors:* enduring factors or conditions which increase risk.	*Protective Factors:* enduring conditions or attributes which decrease risk.
Transient Factors	*Challengers:* transient but significant stresses.	*Buffers:* transient conditions which act as buffers against transient increases in stress or challenge.

Challengers. Included here are the transient challenges or stresses that confront an individual or a family, which may cause a predisposed parent to maltreat his or her child. Significant stressors include loss (of status, economic viability, or a spouse or loved one), physical injury or illness, legal difficulties, marital or family problems, discipline problems with children, and so on. Challengers are stressors that may fluctuate on a short-term basis.

Protective factors. This category includes those relatively enduring or permanent conditions or attributes that decrease the risk of maltreatment or its transmission across generations. Examples of likely protective factors include "desirable" attributes such as good temperament, high intelligence, flexibility and adaptability, good physical health, physical attractiveness and poise, social and interpersonal skills, exceptional talents, good coping and problem-solving skills, a history of good parenting, and so on.

Buffers. Included here are relatively transient factors that may protect or buffer a family from stress or challenge, thereby reducing the probability of maltreatment and its transmission. Probable buffers include substantial financial savings, a good job, a social support system, and so on.

Our proposed model argues that we must examine all categories of risk factors and their transactions over time in order to understand the occurrence and specific form of maltreatment as well as the choice of target (that is, which children are the primary targets of the maltreatment). While there are multiple etiologies for child maltreatment, a vulnerable parent, a vulnerable child, environmental challenge and a relative absence of compensatory protective factors and buffers may be involved in any combination. According to our model, maltreatment is expressed only when potentiating factors override compensatory ones, and some theoretical threshold is crossed. Anything reducing vulnerability or stress, or increasing buffers or protective factors, should decrease the probability of maltreatment and its transmission (Cicchetti and Rizley, 1978).

5. How Is Maltreatment Transmitted Across Generations? We think that transmission can best be understood by examining the transmission of risk factors for child maltreatment—that is, those factors that increase or decrease the probability of maltreatment. Cross-generational transmission must operate by either increasing vulnerability or decreasing protective factors. We are attempting to identify some of the many mechanisms by which risk factors are maintained or perpetuated across generations. More specifically, we are interested in the relationships among the transactive risk factors (both potentiating and compensatory or protective factors) in three generations—grandparents, parents, and children. Additionally, we are studying a subgroup of "high risk" subjects—the siblings of participating maltreating parents. Again, however, we believe that there is no single pathway for transmission across generations. Instead, we must look to the multitude of potentiating and compensatory factors and the specific ways in which they are affected by particular childrearing patterns.

6. How Is Transmission Across Generations Broken? We know that some individuals maltreated as children break the cycle and do not maltreat their own children. What patterns of protective factors are characteristic of parents? Recent research suggests that such factors include a richer network of social connections, different attitudes toward their own children and families, and more detailed recollections and open anger about their own early maltreatment (Hunter and Kilstrom, 1979).

The converse pattern is equally important to study—that is, those parents who were not themselves maltreated in childhood, but who maltreat their own children. These "first generation" occurrences of child maltreatment may prove to be important in revealing unusually deleterious combinations or patterns of risk factors.

Both of these types of intergenerational transmission pattern represent "breaks" in transmission which are particularly informative and which may allow us to test alternative or competing hypotheses regarding the etiology and transmission of maltreatment.

Table 2 clarifies the basic design of the Harvard Child Maltreatment Project as it relates to the intergenerational transmission issues. Using our structured maltreatment interview (Cicchetti, Rizley, Aber, and Carlson-Luden, 1980) and our operational criteria for designation to type of maltreatment in the maltreatment spectrum (Rizley and Cicchetti, 1980c), we are studying four groups of families.

In our nomenclature, those parents who were themselves maltreated as children, but who are not currently maltreating their own children, are classified as *nontransmission parents*. The group of parents who do not appear to have been maltreated themselves during childhood, but who are currently maltreating their own children, are referred to as the *new maltreatment parents*. Both of these groups are compared to yet a third group of *transmission parents*—parents

Table 2. Harvard Child Maltreatment Project Design to Study Patterns of Intergenerational Transmission of Child Maltreatment

		Presence of Maltreatment in the Parents' Upbringing	
		Yes	*No*
Maltreatment in Current Generation	*Yes*	Transmission Parents (2-generation-maltreatment)	New Maltreatment Parents
	No	Nontransmission Parents	Nonmaltreatment Parents (2-generation-nonmaltreatment)

whose histories are characterized by maltreatment across the two most recent generations (that is, parents who were both maltreated themselves as children and who are currently maltreating their own children). A final group included in our study are the *nonmaltreating parents,* characterized by no obvious maltreatment across two consecutive generations—that is, parents who show no evidence of maltreatment either in their own backgrounds or in their current childrearing practices.

In addition, we are studying a subset of the siblings of the parents in each of these four groups. Because they share many of the background risk and protective factors with the maltreatment groups, they provide us with a natural comparison group which may economically illuminate the differential patterns of transmission of risk factors. Siblings may or may not themselves exhibit child maltreatment and they may or may not have been maltreated themselves. Hence they may fall in any of the four cells shown in Table 2. Furthermore, by studying those who meet project criteria for maltreatment of their own children without having been legally identified as such, we can begin to disentangle the effects of legal identification and labeling from those of actual child maltreatment.

A final broad issue which we are addressing in the longitudinal component of the project involves investigating the effects that maltreatment has upon these children's development. Three specific project questions address this important problem.

7. **What Effects Do Different Types of Maltreatment Have on the Child's Social, Emotional, Cognitive and Physical Development?** We are examining carefully the developmental process of the maltreated children in our sample and their siblings in an attempt to identify stage-specific impairments resulting from different forms of maltreatment. Children who have been abused or neglected by their parents may suffer from particularly devastating developmental difficulties in their social relationships, emotional stability, social-cognitive reasoning and emotional development. The identification of these stage-specific problems is the first step towards eventual amelioration through appropriate intervention.

8. **What Factors May Buffer Children from the Deleterious Effects of Maltreatment or Make them More Vulnerable to Its Negative Consequences?** In our investigation of the development of competence in these children, we may discover factors that consistently appear in those children who, despite their history of maltreatment, are socially, emotionally, and cognitively well adapted (see, for example, Garmezy, 1974). Potential buffering or protective factors include a secure attachment relationship with a parent, sibling, or grandparent, status in a particular peer group, or high personal tolerance for stress. Likewise, certain factors may render other children more vulnerable to the effects of maltreatment. The identification of the competent

maltreated child may suggest diagnostic and treatment interventions designed to ameliorate specific disabilities in maltreated children. For example, research may suggest competencies which, if taught to a maltreated child, might reduce the latter's risk for psychopathology or maladaptation.

9. Is Early Maladaptation Resulting from Maltreatment Predictive of Future Developmental Problems? We can do little to answer this question definitively in a three-year longitudinal study. However, the cohort of children and families we are developing during our first three project years will be followed for years to come. The demonstration of continuity in the quality of adaptation or maladaptation, as well as documentation of the reasons for discontinuity in the adaptive or maladaptive process, has important implications for the identification, intervention, and treatment of disturbed families. Moreover, by utilizing broad-band developmental assessments of age-appropriate indices of cognitive, social, and emotional competence, we will be able to answer important questions about the relationship between the successful resolution of the salient tasks of early development and later adaptation (see, for example, Sroufe, 1979a,b). These will be carried out in future cross-sectional and longitudinal studies as we continue to follow our cohort over the years.

In addition to the questions we have addressed in the Harvard Child Maltreatment Project, we are embarking on an additional study within the framework of our existing project—a *prospective investigation* of the etiology, transmission, and sequelae of maltreatment. The existing literature estimates that physical abuse recurs in up to 60 percent of the documented cases. Undoubtedly, other problems in the spectrum of child maltreatment also occur, placing the risk for recidivism at an even higher rate. Thus any knowledge of the antecedent characteristics of child maltreatment will not only enhance our understanding of the causal pathways involved in the etiology, transmission, and developmental sequelae of maltreatment phenomena, but also aid in the formulation of preventive measures to combat the problem of maltreatment. Unlike the existing prospective studies of child maltreatment which have drawn their populations from theoretically "at risk" samples, we have developed a cohort of families where documented maltreatment has already occurred in one or more children and across one or more generations.

Contributions of Developmental Theory to the Problem of Child Maltreatment

We believe that the study of maltreated children can make many significant contributions to our theory of normal development—primarily through contributing precision to developmental theory, affirming it, challenging it, and forcing us to examine our theory of development more critically in relation to our knowledge about psychopathology. Just as is the case with cross-cultural research, another approach to validating the claim of universality of a developmental sequence is to study populations where one might expect on *a priori* grounds to find differing patterns. The results of such empirical and theoretical investigations may be the description of alternative developmental pathways leading to the same or different outcomes of the developmental sequence, and a weighting of the respective roles of, for example, biological, socioemotional, and cognitive-linguistic factors in mental growth. Conversely, before one is capable of grasping deviances that exist in a system, one must also possess an accurate description of the system itself. Furthermore, if, for example, we are to understand the transmission of abnormalities from one developmental level to another, then we must know how the normal transitions from one level of functioning to another are accomplished. Only when we understand the total ongoing development of normal systems can we comprehend developmental deviations as adaptational irregularities of those systems (von Bertalanffy, 1968).

A developmental scheme is also necessary for tracing the roots, etiology, and nature of maladaptation so that treatment interventions may be appropriately timed and guided. Moreover, a developmental perspective will prove useful for uncovering the nature and etiology of the maladaptation, the development of compensatory mechanisms in the face of deficiencies, and the interrelationships between maladaptation and abuse and neglect.

Perhaps the core developmental issue in research with maltreated or high-risk children is the problem of predicting later maladaptation, or, more broadly, the problem of demonstrating continuity in the quality of adaptation across the life span (Kohlberg, Lacrosse, and Ricks, 1972; Santostefano and Baker, 1972). One of the major concerns for primary prevention is predicting those infants and children who are going to have later psychopathology. This is closely related to the problem of assessing early developmental failure. Despite the fact that risk researchers have identified a variety of factors that influence pathological developmental outcomes (see, for example, Garmezy, 1974; Garmezy and Streitman, 1974), we are still unable to predict psychopathology with great accuracy. Moreover, as yet risk research has contributed relatively little to the delineation of continuities between early and later pathology. It is already clear that *homotypic continuity* — symptomatic isomorphism from early childhood on — is not prevalent (Kagan, 1971; Kohlberg, Lacrosse, and Ricks, 1972; Mischel, 1968). The developmental processes underlying pathology are certain to be complex, with early failure related to later pathology in a complicated fashion. When development is depicted as a series of behavioral reorganizations around a series of developmental tasks or issues (Spitz, 1965; Sroufe, 1979b), it becomes possible to define maladaptation in terms of developmental deviation and continuity of adaptation in terms of competence or incompetence across a series of developmentally defined tasks, rather than to pursue static individual consistency. Within an organizational-developmental perspective, the specific pattern of behavior manifested in one situation at a particular developmental level *cannot* be expected to recur in the exact form in either the same or other contexts at later developmental periods. Rather, with development, behaviors are expected to undergo transformation, hierarchical integration, and reorganization (Emde, Gaensbauer, and Harmon, 1976; Serafica, 1978; Sroufe, 1979a). Instead of seeking stability of behavioral expression across time, the organizational viewpoint requires *coherence of patterns* of behavioral organization or adaptation, such that early adaptation is related to later adaptation in a lawful fashion (Block and Block, 1979; Sroufe, 1979b). Within this framework, continuity refers to the prediction that competence in dealing with one developmental issue (for example, the formation of a secure attachment relationship) will be related to competence with respect to subsequent issues (for example, successful integration into and mastery of the peer world). The salient methodological issues are to utilize broad-band, age-appropriate measures of competence and to select age-appropriate situations, each of which elicit a variety of behavioral patterns that are more or less adaptive for that developmental period (Matas, Arend and Sroufe, 1978; Sroufe, 1979b).

The Organismic Perspective of Development

The perspective within which development is viewed greatly influences the interpretation of data on child behavior and growth. It is of paramount importance to formulate a developmental model that is broad enough to guide prospective, longitudinal studies of the processes of adaptation in maltreated as well as nonmaltreated children, and the factors that shape their course (see, for example, Sroufe, 1979b). An adequate model must transcend the simple linear, "main effects" developmental models prevalent in the psychological literature and in the research done in the area of child maltreatment (Reese and Overton, 1970; Sameroff and Chandler, 1975).

Researchers and theoreticians have begun to conceptualize a child's developmental outcomes as having multiple historical and causal determinants rather than single-factor etiologies. Since research in the area of child maltreatment is firmly rooted in medicine, biology, and the "medical" model, it is perhaps understandable why the majority of research in the area has focused upon uncovering *the* cause and *the* outcome of maltreatment phenomena. However, we think that most theoretical depictions of the medical model are inaccurate and overly simplistic, since biology is a dynamic discipline. Hence a true biologic or "medical" model, which we feel would prove to be more accurate, is one in which there is a system breakdown in a dynamic organism-environment transaction (see Piaget, 1971; Sameroff and Chandler, 1975; von Bertalanffy, 1968).

An all-encompassing yet theoretically meaningful model of development must yield a formulation of developmental continuity that can embrace both change and stability (Piaget, 1971; Reese and Overton, 1970; Werner and Kaplan, 1963). Additionally, it must be sufficiently complex to reflect the multifaceted ways in which constitutional, organismic, and environmental factors affect development. For abused and neglected children in particular, growth and development are related to a plethora of factors, particularly the type and severity of maltreatment and the quality of care the child receives (Sameroff and Chandler, 1975).

Sameroff and Chandler (1975) have proposed a biological model that takes into account the interrelationships among dynamic systems and the processes characterizing system breakdown. Moreover, they explain the mechanisms by which compensatory, self-regulating tendencies (Waddington, 1966) are initiated whenever higher-level monitors detect deviances in a subsystem. The transactional model views the multiple transactions among environmental forces, caregiver characteristics, and child characteristics as dynamic, reciprocal contributions to the events and outcomes of child development. This model decries the efficacy of simple, linear "cause-effect" models of causality and suggests that it is impossible to understand a child's development by focusing on single pathogenic events. Rather, Sameroff and Chandler (1975) argue that *how* the environment responds to a particular child's characteristics at a particular time must be analyzed in a dynamic fashion. The transactional model presents the environment and child as mutually influencing. Thus, if a child demonstrates deviant development across time it is assumed that the child has been involved in a *continuous* maladaptive process. The continued manifestation of maladaptation depends on environmental support, while the child's characteristics, reciprocally, determine the nature of the environment.

Sameroff and Chandler's (1975) proposal that we consider a child's position on both the "continuum of reproductive casualty" and the "continuum of caretaking casualty" has obvious applications to the study of the developmental sequelae of maltreated children. Since maltreated children are at different points along the continua of "caretaking" and "repreductive" casualty, it is not surprising that we would find both between- and within-group differences in developmental outcome. Thus, the transactional developmental perspective makes it plausible to view maltreatment phenomena as expressions of an underlying dysfunction in the parent-child-environment system, rather than solely the result of aberrant parental personality traits, environmental stress or deviant child characteristics. From the viewpoint of a transactional model, it is clear that temporal continuity of patterns of behavioral organization is to be sought (what Kagan (1971) has called *heterotypic continuity*) rather than temporal stability of the frequency of discrete behaviors. Since the child and the environment are seen as reciprocally influencing, it follows that behavior at a later point reflects not only the quality of earlier adaptation but also the intervening environmental inputs and supports. As time elapses, and as the child develops, both the match between child and parent as well as salient parent characteristics may change. The maladapted child in ways creates its own environment and may contribute to its own developmental anomalies. In such a case a declining quality of adaptation would demonstrate continuity of development (Egeland and Sroufe, this volume; Sroufe, 1979a). Such a holistic, biological model is congruent with the theoretical conceptualizations of organismic theorists in the field of developmental psychology (Piaget, 1971; Reese and Overton, 1970; Sroufe, 1979a; Werner, 1948; White, 1976).

We believe that the study of maltreated children and their families is not only a legitimate enterprise for developmental psychologists, but also one that merits highest research priority. As we have shown, the developmental approach can make invaluable contributions to our understanding of maltreatment phenomena. Moreover, empirical investigations of the developmental processes and sequelae of maltreated children will enhance our theoretical understanding of normal development.

The study of maltreated children and their families has an urgency characteristic of all research that touches upon great problems of social concern. Researchers and practitioners must redouble their efforts if these families are ever to receive the comprehensive high-quality intervention necessary for the eradication of this insidious problem.

Summary

We have underscored the many practical research problems facing those involved in the scientific study of child maltreatment. In addition, we have discussed several conceptual complexities that have not been fully acknowledged or addressed to date. We are committed to the idea that research in this area must reflect the true complexity of the phenomena itself. It is our hope that continued funding and interest in the problem of maltreatment, coupled with continuing sophistication in our theory and research techniques, will move us rapidly toward a comprehensive and integrative understanding of this important social problem. The challenge facing us all is to make full use of the most recent advances—theoretical, methodological, and empirical—in the areas of developmental psychology, psychopathology, psychiatric nosology and measurement, adult and child personality development, family/social systems theory, experimental design and mathematical statistical modelling. While current approaches have proven useful and heuristic, there must be continued interaction and cross-fertilization between researchers and theorists concerned with child maltreatment and those in other areas of psychology or psychiatry. The failure to make use of the most sophisticated empirical and conceptual tools available can no longer be justified.

References

Altemeier, W. A. *Causal Factors in Neglect and Battering: A Prospective Study.* Final report submitted to the National Center on Child Abuse and Neglect, Administration for Children, Youth, and Families, U.S. Department of Health, Education, and Welfare, December, 1978.

Belsky, J. "Child Maltreatment: An Ecological Integration." *American Psychologist,* 1980, *35,* 320–335.

Bertalanffy, L. von. *General System Theory.* New York: Braziller, 1968.

Block, J. H., and Block, J. "The Role of Ego-Control and Ego-Resiliency in the Organization of Behavior." In W. A. Collins (Ed.), *Minnesota Symposium on Child Psychology.* Vol. 13. Hillsdale, N.J.: Erlbaum, 1979.

Bronfenbrenner, U. "Toward an Experimental Ecology of Human Development." *American Psychologist,* 1977, *32,* 513–531.

Bronfenbrenner, U. *The Ecology of Human Development.* Cambridge, Mass.: Harvard University Press, 1979.

Bruner, J., Oliver, R., and Greenfield, P. *Studies in Cognitive Growth.* New York: Wiley, 1966.

Cicchetti, D., and Aber, J. L. "Abused Children—Abusive Parents: An Overstated Case?" *Harvard Educational Review,* 1980, *50,* 244–255.

Cicchetti, D., and Rizley, R. *The Etiology, Transmission, and Sequelae of Child Maltreatment: Toward a Three-Dimensional Threshold Transactional Model.* Grant proposal, Department of Health, Education, and Welfare, 1978.

Cicchetti, D., Rizley, R., Aber, L., and Carlson-Luden, V. *The Maltreatment Classification Interview: A Structured Interview to Assess Current and Past Child Maltreatment.* Harvard University, 1980.

Cicchetti, D., and Sroufe, L. A. "An Organizational View of Affect: Illustration from the Study of Down's Syndrome Infants." In M. Lewis and L. Rosenblum (Eds.), *The Development of Affect.* New York: Plenum Press, 1978.

Cicchetti, D., Taraldson, B., and Egeland, B. "Perspectives in the Treatment and Understanding of Child Abuse." In A. Goldstein (Ed.) *Prescriptions for Child Mental Health and Education.* Elmsford, N.Y.: Pergamon Press, 1978.

Egeland, B., and Brunnquell, D. "An At-Risk Approach to the Study of Child Abuse: Some Preliminary Findings." *Journal of the American Academy of Child Psychiatry,* 1979, *18,* 219–235.

Elmer, E. *Fragile Families, Troubled Children.* Pittsburgh: University of Pittsburgh Press, 1977.

Emde, R., Gaensbauer, T., and Harmon, R. *Emotional Expression in Infancy: A Biobehavioral Study.* New York: International Universities Press, 1976.

Fiske, D. W. "The Limits for the Conventional Science of Personality." *Journal of Personality,* 1974, *42,* 1–11.

Furman, W., Rahe, D., and Hartup, W. "Rehabilitation of Socially Withdrawn Preschool Children through Mixed-Age and Same-Age Socialization." *Child Development,* 1979, *50,* 915–922.

Gaensbauer, T. J., and Sands, S. K. "Distorted Affective Communications in Abused/Neglected Infants and Their Potential Impact on Caretakers." *Journal of the American Academy of Child Psychiatry,* 1979, *18,* 236–250.

Garbarino, J. "A Preliminary Study of Some Ecological Correlates of Child Abuse: The Impact of Socio-Economic Stress on Mothers." *Child Development,* 1976, *47,* 178–185.

Garbarino, J. "The Human Ecology of Child Maltreatment: A Conceptual Model for Research." *Journal of Marriage and the Family,* 1977, *39,* 721–736.

Garbarino, J., and Crouter, A. "Defining the Community Context for Parent-Child Relations: The Correlates of Child Maltreatment." *Child Development,* 1978, *49,* 604–616.

Garmezy, N. "The Study of Competence in Children at Risk for Severe Psychopathology." In E. J. Anthony and C. Koupernik (Eds.), *The Child in His Family.* New York: Wiley, 1974.

Garmezy, N., and Streitman, S. "Children at Risk: The Search for the Antecedents of Schizophrenia." Part 1: "Conceptual Models and Research Methods." *Schizophrenia Bulletin,* 1974, *8,* 14–90.

Gelles, R. "Child Abuse as Psychopathology: A Sociological Critique and Reformulation." *American Journal of Orthopsychiatry,* 1973, *43,* 611–621.

Gelles, R. "Violence toward Children in the United States." *American Journal of Orthopsychiatry,* 1978, *48,* 580–592.

Gelles, R. "A Profile of Violence toward Children in the United States." In G. Gerbner, C. J. Ross, and E. Zigler (Eds.), *Child Abuse: An Agenda for Action.* New York: Oxford University Press, 1980.

George, C., and Main, M. "Social Interactions of Young Abused Children: Approach, Avoidance, and Aggression." *Child Development,* 1979, *50,* 306–318.

Gil, D. *Violence Against Children: Physical Child Abuse in the United States.* Cambridge, Mass.: Harvard University Press, 1970.

Giovannoni, J. M., and Becerra, R. M. *Defining Child Abuse.* New York: Free Press, 1979.

Goldstein, J., Freud, A., and Solnit, A. *Beyond the Best Interests of the Child.* New York: Free Press, 1973.

Goldstein, J., Freud, A., and Solnit, A. *Before the Best Interests of the Child.* New York: Free Press, 1979.

Gordon, A., and Jameson, J. "Infant-Mother Attachment in Patients with Nonorganic Failure-to-Thrive Syndrome." *Journal of the American Academy of Child Psychiatry,* 1979, *18,* 251–259.

Hunter, R. S., and Kilstrom, N. "Breaking the Cycle in Abusive Families." *American Journal of Psychiatry,* 1979, *136,* 1320–1322.

Hunter, R. S., Kilstrom, N., Kraybill, E. N., and Loda, F. "Antecedents of Child Abuse and Neglect in Premature Infants: A Prospective Study in a Newborn Intensive Care Unit." *Pediatrics,* 1978, *61,* 629–635.

Kagan, J. *Change and Continuity in Infancy.* New York: Wiley, 1971.

Kempe, C. H., and Helfer, R. (Eds.). *Helping the Battered Child and His Family.* Philadelphia: Lippincott, 1972.

Kempe, R., and Kempe, C. H. *Child Abuse.* Cambridge, Mass.: Harvard University Press, 1978.

Kent, J. "A Follow-Up Study of Abused Children." *Journal of Pediatric Psychology,* 1976, *1,* 25–31.

Kinard, E. M. "Emotional Development in Physically Abused Children." *American Journal of Orthopsychiatry,* 1980, *50,* 686–696.

Kohlberg, L., Lacrosse, J., and Ricks, D. "The Predictability of Adult Mental Health." In B. Wolman (Ed.), *Manual of Child Psychopathology.* New York: Wiley, 1972.

Light, R. "Abused and Neglected Children in America: A Study of Alternative Policies." *Harvard Educational Review,* 1973, *43,* 556–598.

Martin, H. P. (Ed.). *The Abused Child: Multidisciplinary Approach to Developmental Issues and Treatment.* Cambridge, Mass.: Ballinger, 1976.

Martin, H. P., and Beezeley, P. "Behavioral Observations of Abused Children." *Developmental Medicine and Child Neurology,* 1977, *19,* 373–387.

54

Matas, L., Arend, R. A., and Sroufe, L. A. "Continuity of Adaptation in the Second Year: The Relationship Between Quality of Attachment and Later Competence." *Child Development,* 1978, *49,* 547-556.

Meehl, P. E. "Nuisance Variables and the Ex Post Facto Design." In M. Radner and S. Winokur (Eds.), *Minnesota Studies in the Philosophy of Science,* Vol. 4. Minneapolis: University of Minnesota Press, 1970.

Mischel, W. *Personality and Assessment.* New York: Wiley, 1968.

Nagi, S. Z. *Child Maltreatment in the United States.* New York: Columbia University Press, 1977.

O'Connor, S., Altemeier, W., and Sherrod, K., Sandler, H., and Vietze, P. *Prospective Study of Non-organic Failure To Thrive.* Paper presented at the biennial meeting of the Society for Research in Child Development, San Francisco, April 1979.

Parke, R. D., and Collmer, C. W. "Child Abuse: An Interdisciplinary Analysis." In E. M. Hetherington (Ed.), *Review of Child Development Research.* Vol. 5. Chicago: University of Chicago Press, 1975.

Piaget, J. *Biology and Knowledge.* Chicago: University of Chicago Press, 1971.

Radbill, S. "A History of Child Abuse and Infanticide." In R. Helfer and C. H. Kempe (Eds.), *The Battered Child.* Chicago: University of Chicago Press, 1968.

Reese, H., and Overton, W. "Models of Development and Theories of Development. In L. R. Goulet and P. Baltes (Eds.), *Life-Span Developmental Psychology: Research and Theory.* New York: Academic Press, 1970.

Reidy, T. "The Aggressive Characteristics of Abused and Neglected Children." *Journal of Clinical Psychology,* 1977, *33,* 1140-1145.

Rizley, R., and Cicchetti, D. *Heterogeneity in the Etiology, Type, Sequelae, and Treatment of Child Maltreatment.* Unpublished manuscript, Harvard University, 1980a.

Rizley, R., and Cicchetti, D. *The Construct Validation of a Nosology for Child Maltreatment.* Unpublished manuscript, Harvard University, 1980b.

Rizley, R., and Cicchetti, D. *Research Criteria And Structured Assessments for Child Maltreatment.* Unpublished manuscript, Harvard University, 1980c.

Robins, L., Helzer, J., Croughan, J., and Spitzer, R. *The NIMH Diagnostic Interview Schedule (DIS), Version 2.* Washington, D.C.: National Institute of Mental Health, 1979.

Ross, C. J. "The Lessons of the Past: Defining and Controlling Child Abuse in the United States." In G. Gerbner, C. J. Ross, and E. Zigler (Eds.), *Child Abuse: An Agenda for Action.* New York: Oxford University Press, 1980.

Sameroff, A., and Chandler, M. "Reproductive Risk and the Continuum of Caretaking Casualty." In F. Horowitz (Ed.), *Review of Child Development Research.* Vol. 4. Chicago: University of Chicago Press, 1975.

Santostefano, S., and Baker, A. H. "The Contribution of Developmental Psychology." In B. Wolman (Ed.), *Manual of Child Psychopathology.* New York: Wiley, 1972.

Serafica, F. C. "The Development of Attachment Behaviors: An Organismic-Developmental Perspective." *Human Development,* 1978, *21,* 119-140.

Solnit, A. "Too Much Reporting, Too Little Service: Roots and Prevention of Child Abuse." In G. Gerbner, C. Ross, and E. Zigler (Eds.), *Child Abuse: An Agenda for Action.* New York: Oxford University Press, 1980.

Spinetta, J., and Rigler, D. "The Child-Abusing Parent: A Psychological Review." *Psychological Bulletin,* 1972, *77,* 296-304.

Spitz, R. *The First Year of Life.* New York: International Universities Press, 1965.

Spitzer, R. L., and Endicott, J. *Schedule for Affective Disorders and Schizophrenia.* New York: Biometrics Research Division, New York State Psychiatric Institute, 1978a.

Spitzer, R. L., and Endicott, J. *Schedule for Affective Disorders and Schizophrenia — Life-time Version.* New York: Biometrics Research Division, New York State Psychiatric Institute, 1978b.

Spitzer, R. L., Endicott, J., and Robins, E. "Research Diagnostic Criteria: Rationale and Reliability." *Archives of General Psychiatry,* 1978, *35,* 773–782a.
Spitzer, R. L., Endicott, J., and Robins, E. *Research Diagnostic Criteria (RDC).* New York: Biometrics Research Division, New York State Psychiatric Institute, 1978b.
Sroufe, L. A. "Socioemotional Development." In J. Osofsky (Ed.), *Handbook of Infant Development.* New York: Wiley, 1979a.
Sroufe, L. A. "The Coherence of Individual Development." *American Psychologist,* 1979b, *34,* 834–841.
Starr, R., Ceresnie, S., and Rossi, J. "What Child Abuse Researchers Don't Tell About Child Abuse Research." *Pediatric Psychology,* 1976, *1,* 50–53.
Terr, L. "A Family Study of Child Abuse." *American Journal of Psychiatry,* 1970, *127,* 665–671.
Waddington, C. H. *Principles of Development and Differentiation.* New York: Macmillan, 1966.
Wald, M. "State Intervention on Behalf of 'Neglected' Children: Standards for Removal of Children from Their Homes, Monitoring the Status of Children in Foster Care, and Termination of Parental Rights." *Stanford Law Review,* 1976, *28,* 623–707.
Werner, H. "Process and Achievement: A Basic Problem of Education and Developmental Psychology." *Harvard Educational Review,* 1937, *7,* 353–368.
Werner, H. *Comparative Psychology of Mental Development.* Chicago: Follett, 1948.
Werner, H., and Kaplan, B. *Symbol Formation.* New York: Wiley, 1963.
White, S. H. "The Active Organism in Theoretical Behaviorism." *Human Development,* 1976, *19,* 99–107.
Yarrow, M., Campbell, J., and Burton, R. "Recollections of Childhood: A Study of the Retrospective Method." *Monographs of the Society for Research in Child Development,* 1970, *35,* Serial No. 138.
Zigler, E. "Controlling Child Abuse: An Effort Doomed to Failure?" In W. A. Collins (Ed.), *Newsletter of the Division on Developmental Psychology, American Psychological Association,* February, 1976, 17–30.

Dante Cicchetti is an assistant professor of psychology and social relations at Harvard University where he is co-director of the Developmental Risk Research Project and the Harvard Child Maltreatment Project.

Ross Rizley is an assistant professor of psychology and social relations at Harvard University where he is co-director of the Developmental Risk Research Project and the Harvard Child Maltreatment Project.

Antecedents and consequences of child maltreatment are viewed within an ecological framework as the product of ineffective attempts to cope with intrapersonal, intrafamilial, and extrafamilial sources of frustration and conflict. Long-term effects of the abusive environment and foster care on the development of the abused child are discussed.

Some Antecedents and Developmental Consequences of Child Maltreatment

Roy C. Herrenkohl
Ellen C. Herrenkohl

Description of Research

Over the past decade or two, a growing body of research has delineated the nature and scope of child maltreatment; however, our understanding of the antecedents and consequences of child maltreatment remains fragmented. As a result, it is unclear how to focus services to accomplish objectives such as reducing the effects of maltreatment on children, reducing the amount of repeated abuse, and eventually preventing the occurrence of maltreatment.

The understanding and prediction of child maltreatment relies on more than knowledge of the environment and personal history of any parent.

The authors wish to thank the Lehigh County (Penn.) Office of Children and Youth Services and the Northampton County (Penn.) Children and Youth Division for their cooperation. Portions of the research reported here were funded by the Administration on Children, Youth, and Families, National Center on Child Abuse and Neglect, (Contract Nos. 90-C428 and 90-C-1831) and by the National Institute of Mental Health, Grant No. 1-R01-MH26291.

It requires, in addition, an integrated understanding of the family structural system, the social and cultural context of the family, the stresses experienced by family members, and the strategies used to cope with those stresses. Research data which would lend itself to substantiation of an integrative model have previously been lacking. This paper attempts to begin such a documentation.

The research reported here consists of three projects conducted in a two-county area of eastern Pennsylvania. A retrospective study referred to as the "follow-up study" involved all families (N = 328) who were charged with child maltreatment over a ten-year period (1967–1976) in the two-county area. The objective was to determine the frequency of repeated maltreatment as indicated by the child welfare case records and to assess characteristics associated with repeated maltreatment by means of an interview.

The *analysis of case records* for all 328 families covered demographic characteristics, family relationships, household changes such as child placements, stresses, health and emotional problems, and services received. Also involved was the analysis of 3,719 incidents of maltreatment, nonabusive discipline, accidents, and adult conflict. These provided evidence for extent of repeated maltreatment.

The demographic characteristics of the families were: 83.0 percent white, 12.0 percent Spanish surname, and 5.0 percent Black; 62.0 percent Protestant, 24.0 percent Catholic, and less than one percent Jewish; 86.0 percent with both a male and female head, although not necessarily married; 34.5 percent of the female heads and 31.4 percent of the male heads with at least a high school education; and 19.2 percent of the families interviewed living in public housing.

The frequency of different types of maltreatment was found to be: physical abuse, 79.0 percent; emotional abuse, 13.0 percent; sexual abuse, 8.0 percent; and gross neglect, 25.0 percent. These proportions add up to more than 100 percent because approximately one-third of the families were involved in more than one type of maltreatment. In 13.0 percent of the families there was no verifiable incident, and the charge was considered invalid. While the rate could vary depending on the criteria used, repeated maltreatment was identified in as many as 66.0 percent of the families with one incident.

The *interview* was done with those parents who would agree to participate. One hundred fifty-one female heads and sixty-six male heads participated. The percentage of families with single and multiple incidents of maltreatment was approximately the same among the families agreeing to interviews and the total group of maltreating families. Families with no validated incident of maltreatment were not contacted. The interview covered topics suggested by the literature as having possible relevance to understanding the occurrence of child maltreatment. Topics covered were: demographic characteristics, family relationships, employment history, income level, use of community resources,

sources of stress, physical and emotional problems, quality of housing, quality of neighborhood, quality of parent-child relationships (including views on childrearing, childrearing problems and concerns, and expectations of child development), discipline practices and norms of discipline, quality of marital relationships, and parents' perceptions of their own childrearing. The interviewer also completed a rating scale on the family, which included items from Polansky's (1972) level-of-living scale.

Permission was requested from each parent interviewed to examine the child's hospital birth records. Wherever the information was provided, the following issues were coded: weeks of gestation at birth, age of mother at child's birth, birth weight, Apgar scores, complications associated with pregnancy, complications associated with the delivery, and any problems or abnormalities of the baby noted by the medical staff. While recent studies of newborns have used such comprehensive and sensitive measures of infant characteristics as the Brazelton Scale (1973), such information was not available in these birth records.

The second study, referred to as the "coping study," examined the *family coping strategies* of both maltreating and nonmaltreating families with preschool children aged eighteen through seventy-one months. A focal group of families had one or more maltreated children and had received less than a year of child welfare services (N = 72). Three control groups were selected: a group of nonmaltreating, protective service families served by the child welfare agency (N = 74), a group of nonchild welfare families served by Head Start (N = 50), and a group of nonchild welfare families served by daycare programs (N = 50).

The protective service families were of slightly lower average financial status than the maltreatment group, while the Head Start families were still lower. The daycare group had the highest income level. Approximately one-third (36 percent) of the daycare families had more than a $10,000 annual income.

The focus of the coping study was the quality of the parent-child interaction. The objective was assessment of the quality of the interaction, identification of the factors in the family which affected it, and determination of the relationship of the quality of interaction to the child's cognitive and social functioning.

Observations of structured parent-child interactions were done in the home by two observers, one observing the parent and another observing the child. The parent and child worked on four tasks (puzzle, play-doh, felt board, and story reading) selected because they tended to elicit a variety of behaviors: achievement orientation, affection, verbal and nonverbal interaction. The observers recorded the occurrence during ten-second intervals of eighteen nonverbal behaviors (for example, smiling, helping, eye contact) while parent and child played together on four five-minute tasks. The verbal behavior of parent and child was recorded on tape for later analysis. Verbal behavior was coded in twelve categories (for example, approval, criticism, directing).

The *interview* instrument used in the follow-up study was also used in this study with mother or surrogate mother and, where possible, with the father or surrogate father. *Hospital records* of the child were also obtained and analyzed as described above. *Cognitive functioning* of the child was assessed in the home with the McCarthy Scales of Cognitive Abilities. *Free-play behavior of the child in the preschool classroom* was observed on two occasions a week apart. Ratings of the behavior were made using a scale which represented a revised and expanded version of the Emmerich personal-social constructs list (1971). This includes behaviors such as aggression or withdrawal reactions to frustration, leadership of others, withdrawal from others, and task-oriented behaviors. A *behavior checklist* was completed by the child's teacher. This included assessment of behavior such as fine and gross motor coordination, leadership among peers, and dependency on the adult.

The third study is a *longitudinal study,* begun in 1979, and referred to as the "longitudinal study." It was designed to follow up on all families studied previously in the coping study (N = 246) and a portion of the families studied in the follow-up study (N = 59). To provide a broader range, an additional middle-income control group (N = 52) was added to the low-income control groups of the coping study, bringing the total number of families to 357.

The focus of this study is the longer-term consequences for the children of the maltreating environment. The objective is to relate what was learned from the coping study about the child's functioning in preschool years, the parent-child interaction, and other qualities of the family environment to the development of the child as assessed four years later.

Again, a variety of data collection measures are being used. An *interview* with one, or where possible, both parents combines elements from the earlier follow-up study interview (for example, family composition, services, stresses, separations, finances, health) with new elements. Some of the new components of the interview are: parental reactions to any foster placement of children; perceptions of family conflict and disruption; strategies used in coping with partners; and an extensive set of items to assess locus of control, fear of failure, concern about failing in primary roles, including that of parent, and inability to meet family expectations.

A *child behavior inventory* is completed by the parent at the time of the interview. This inventory includes items from several checklists designed to assess social competence as well as items designed to cover other areas denoted by the literature as being part of social competence (Achenbach, 1978; Achenbach and Edelbrock, 1979; Zigler and Trickett, 1978).

Parent-child interactions are being observed and assessed as before, with revised procedures to accommodate the older age of the children and with modest adjustments in the coding system. The Rosenzweig Picture Frustration Test (Rosenzweig, 1978) is administered to parent and child following the interaction. *Cognitive testing* of the child is done in the home using the WISC-R. *The child's school records* are read and coded, and a teacher who knows the child completes a copy of the child behavior inventory described above.

The child's grandparents are also being interviewed in this study in order to obtain information on the parent as child, from the perspective of their parents, and to provide data on childrearing practices across two generations. The family's *child's welfare record* analysis will be updated, if the family has received child welfare service since the first interview.

The data set resulting from these studies is sizable and multicontextual in nature. One of the criticisms of much child maltreatment research has been its focus on single factors (Garbarino, 1977). The studies reported here, by contrast, are complex, multifactored in their focus, and involve in-depth analyses of a large number of families using both retrospective and prospective approaches. The depth and variety of the data create a major analysis problem since there is a need to achieve a reduced and focused data set without losing valuable information. Initially the process has been an examination of relatively small parts of the overall data set. The results of these initial analyses provide preliminary suggestions of relationships among variables, indications of variables that might be combined to achieve conceptually broader variables, and indication of variables that should serve as statistical controls when examining each of the major issues of the research. The current, long-range data-analysis strategy is to continue data reduction until psychometrically sound variables are achieved, and to organize the variables in accordance with an "ecological model" of child abuse (Belsky, 1980; Bronfenbrenner, 1977; Garbarino, 1977; Garbarino and Stocking, 1980). Such an approach posits interacting influences on behavior from individual, family, community, and cultural sources. Furthermore, life-span development involves mutual accommodation between a developing organism and its changing environments.

The results reported below are based on analyses of portions of data from the follow-up and coping studies. They represent the first steps in the long-range plan to test the explanatory power of an ecological model of child maltreatment. In part, these results provide confirmation of findings of others (Egeland and Brunnquell, 1979; Egeland, Breitenbucher and Rosenberg, 1980; Gelles, 1973) with regard to the association between stress, being a teenage parent, or caring for a premature infant, and the increased risk for maltreatment. Additional findings throw light on the circumstances surrounding the maltreatment incident, and developmental implications of both the mal-

treating environment and certain intervention services for the child victims —
relatively unexplored dimensions of this topic in the research findings reported
to date.

Defining Maltreatment

Giovannoni and Becerra (1979) state that "the task of defining child
abuse and neglect . . . is the setting of criteria or boundaries for specifying
what does and what does not belong in the classification" (p. 19). The follow-
up study afforded an opportunity to utilize one definitional approach — that is,
to identify retrospectively the acts and their results that were labeled "abusive"
by social agencies and authorities responsible for child welfare.

The first step was to examine formal charges or citations of maltreatment to identify the types of acts and their results that were legally defined as
maltreatment. Based on this analysis, lists were developed for each type of
maltreatment. *Physical abuse* involved burning, biting, shooting, and stabbing,
as well as beatings and spankings that left injuries such as bruises or fractures.
Gross neglect included evidence of the "failure-to-thrive syndrome" or depriving
children of crucial medical or nutritional care. *Sexual abuse* involved sexual
molestation of a child by an adult. Sexual abuse was not included in many
subsequent statistical analyses due to insufficient occurrences noted in the case
records to provide reliable results. *Emotional abuse* was added to these categories. Although there was only one case of a citation for emotional abuse, numerous incidents of emotional cruelty were depicted in the case records. Emotional abuse was added to the above types of maltreatment and was defined
conservatively by the investigators to include threats by caretakers to kill or
abandon a child, or attempts to terrify a child by such behaviors as locking in a
closet.

Using these lists as a basis for inclusion in each maltreatment category,
a systematic search of the case record file was made to identify all incidents
toward children that were similar to those on the list. This process provided
the basis for determining whether a family had one or more incidents of maltreatment.

Antecedents of Maltreatment

Explanations of the "sufficient conditions" for the occurrence of child
maltreatment are notable for their number and variety (see, for example,
Parke and Collmer, 1975). Several such explanations are considered below.

Caregiver's Age. Recent research has indicated that teenage pregnancy
has a high likelihood of being premarital and unplanned, and of creating serious financial strains if it leads to marriage (Furstenberg, 1976; Russell, 1980).

While personal growth and greater family organization are possible outcomes of the crisis produced by teenage pregnancy (Russell, 1980), disruption of the family organization and of personal development are problematic consequences for many. The younger the mother, the higher the incidents of marital disruption, poverty, and low educational achievement (Russell, 1980). In the area of personal growth, a teenage parent is confronted with many developmental tasks simultaneously: crystalizing of identity, development of the capacity for intimate relationships, and issues of generativity (Erikson, 1950). These tasks would be more smoothly and successfully dealt with if they were confronted one at a time and in orderly succession.

In the follow-up study, a relationship was found between age of the mother at the time of the child's birth and subsequent physical abuse of the child ($r = -.17$, $p < .01$), and between mother's age and the recurrence of gross neglect of the child ($r = -.13$, $p < .01$) (Herrenkohl and Herrenkohl, 1979a). The younger the mother the more incidents of physical abuse and gross neglect. The correlation between the mother's being under twenty at the time of the child's birth and the number of subsequent physical abuse incidents of the child was $r = .30$ ($p = .001$); the correlation with subsequent incidents of gross neglect was $r = .12$ ($p < .05$).

Egeland and Brunnquell (1979), in their study of infants at risk for child maltreatment, likewise found that the mean age of low-income primiparous mothers who were later identified as irresponsible parents was 19.3 years as opposed to a mean age of 24.5 years among low-income primiparous women later found to be adequate caretakers. Inadequate parenting and abusive childrearing techniques appear to be manifestations of the crises experienced by some teenage parents.

Stress. Probably the most generally held explanation for child maltreatment is that the family or the individual was under stress and as a result, mistreated their child or children. Egeland and Brunnquell (1979) and Egeland, Breitenbucher, and Rosenberg (1980) have referred to the greater extent of disorganization in the lives of inadequate mothers as compared to adequate mothers. The former appear to be less capable of removing themselves from problematic or "hassling" circumstances as well as less skilled in preventing further difficulties. Thus, more environmental obstacles which are overcome by adequate parents develop into major stresses for inadequate parents.

As part of our interview, respondents were asked to rate the extent of stress on the family in thirty-nine areas, including health problems, housing problems, income problems, and family conflict. It was found that the total number of the maltreatment incidents noted in the records of a family is directly related to the total number of stresses on the family as perceived by the respondents ($r = .16$, $p < .05$).

In their transactional model of coping theory and coping skills, Roskies and Lazarus (1980) present broad-based evidence to support the notion that individuals not only respond to the environmental pressures on them, but also shape the stress experience itself. The coping process involves cognitive appraisals of the potentially stressful event as well as the person's coping resources, and of specific coping skills.

In the longitudinal study now in operation, additional exploration of the ability to cope with problems is one major focus. Respondents are questioned about their coping strategies for perceived stresses, and the extent to which these have been put into operation. In addition, the Rosenzweig Picture Frustration Test (1978) is administered as a measure of general response tendencies to frustrating circumstances. These data should throw some light on the extent to which family heads who feel helpless or bereft of coping resources perceive the environment as more stressful as well as the ways in which disorganized approaches to problem solving increase the stress to which the family is subject.

Marital Conflict. The family is the basic social system through which the child learns "the basic social roles, the value of social institutions, and the basic mores of the society" (Lidz, 1970, p. 26). The interrelatedness of the parent-child subsystem of the family unit is reflected in research findings that positive support within the mother-father relationship is associated with competent, sensitive, and affectionate mother-infant relationships, while high conflict in the parent dyad is associated with negative interactions between parent and child (Hetherington and Parke, 1979).

Nearly half (44.0 percent) of the 328 families in the follow-up study had at least one incident of physical conflict recorded (in the case records) between or involving adult family members, and approximately one-fourth (24.0 percent) had more than one incident of conflict between or involving adult family members. Beatings severe enough to leave bruises were the most frequently used method of violence towards adult family members, and occurred in 22.9 percent of the families. More serious physical violence occurred in a smaller proportion of the families.

The greater the frequency of all types of child maltreatment, the greater the frequency of violence toward adult family members ($r = .28$, $p < .01$), and the greater the variety of abusive methods used toward adult family members ($r = .21$, $p < .01$). It would appear that for some families child maltreatment is not an isolated phenomenon but an extension of the climate of violence in their lives (see Straus, Gelles, and Steinmetz, 1980). These findings support the notion that a general tolerance for violence increases the risk of one form of such violence: child abuse (Belsky, 1980; Garbarino, 1977).

In addition to a general cultural toleration of violence in American life as a precipitating factor of family violence, the developmental crises experienced by immature individuals who have been thrust into a parenting role dis-

cussed above may be additional causative agents. For example, Egeland, Breitenbucher, and Rosenberg (1980) and Justice and Justice (1976) point to failure in the process of individuation in the parent's psychological development
as a major source of vulnerability in subsequent functioning as a spouse and as
a parent. Maltreating parents are in competition with other family members
for care and attention, fail to differentiate themselves from others, or become
focused on fusing themselves with others. As a result, considerable tension is
generated within the family; anger results from the desperate and often insa-
tiable needs for care and from the suppression of the opposing drive for individuation. Aggression toward the child may represent a displacement of anger
resulting from such frustration, as well as a safe outlet for the hostility of the
victim of spouse abuse (Parke, 1980).

Future analyses of the follow-up and longitudinal studies will allow
exploration of the degree to which histories of maltreatment in the lives of the
parents themselves, teenage parenting, and family violence are associated.

Characteristics of the Child. Contradictory findings have been reported
about relationship between congenital physical abnormalities in the child and
subsequent maltreatment, with some researchers reporting a relationship and
others reporting no relationship (Friedrich and Boriskin, 1976; Smith, 1976).
Among the 314 children in the follow-up study for whom birth records were
available (Herrenkohl and Herrenkohl, 1979a), no relationship was found
between physical defects of the baby at birth according to hospital records, and
subsequent maltreatment. Although more babies with low Apgar scores were
among those who subsequently suffered gross neglect, this was not a statistically significant relationship. Premature babies were at greater risk for some
types of subsequent maltreatment ($r = .13$, $p < .05$), although the correlations
with any one type of maltreatment were not statistically significant. It appears
that babies who may be sluggish in responding, or who present initial difficulties in care, may fail to elicit strong nurturant responses from their parents, or
evoke negative responses.

Parent's Perceptions of the Child as Different. While some research
(Friedrich and Boriskin, 1976) has lent support to the notion that one child in
a family is singled out for maltreatment as the family scapegoat, the present
study found, to the contrary, that almost half (46.5 percent) of the families in
the abusive population had more than one target of maltreatment, and one-
fifth (20.6 percent) had more than two targets of maltreatment (that is, maltreatment of any type). Those children who were targets of maltreatment were
described by their mothers as having exhibited more types of difficulties in
their development ($r = .20$, $p < .01$), and specifically more emotional difficulties ($r = .21$, $p < .01$), (for example, sleeping and eating problems, frequent
tempter tantrums) (Herrenkohl and Herrenkohl, 1979a). The targets of physical abuse also tended to be described by their mothers as having physical, per-

sonality, or behavior characteristics that reminded them of relatives or of themselves in negative ways. Our findings underscore the fact that maltreated children are perceived by their mothers to be "difficult" children.

Quality of the Parent-Child Interaction

Circumstances under which Maltreatment Occurs. Analyses to date have revealed that the amount and pervasiveness of maltreatment in these families is greater than expected. In addition to the findings that as many as two-thirds of the families with one incident had repeated incidents, it was found that almost half (45.0 percent) of the families have more than one care-taking adult known to maltreat and almost half (46.5 percent) have more than one child maltreated. Furthermore, in one-third (33.5 percent) of the families more than one type of maltreatment was found to have occurred (Herrenkohl, Herrenkohl, Egolf, and Seech, 1979).

Little attention has been paid to the circumstances under which maltreatment occurs (Simkins and others, 1979). Identifying the circumstances surrounding different types of maltreatment may reveal something about why the maltreatment occurs and how it can be prevented.

The small amount of existing evidence, generally unspecified as to type of maltreatment, suggests that maltreatment is often associated with some sort of family crisis. Kempe and Kempe (1978) state "When a child is abused it is always at a point of crisis, often an apparently trivial one . . . the most frequent irritants are messy feeding, soiling (particularly where a parent's clothes get soiled), and intractable crying" (p. 21). Gil (1970) and Justice and Justice (1976) note that maltreatment takes place most frequently around dinner time. Thompson and others (1970) found that three-fifths (57.0 percent) of maltreatment incidents followed rather normal acts of the child (for example, crying, failure to eat, or wetting the bed), while only 10.0 percent followed more serious acts of misconduct such as stealing or running away.

In the case records, examined as part of the follow-up study, reasons for the occurrence of maltreatment and nonmaltreatment incidents were given (Herrenkohl, Herrenkohl, and Egolf, in preparation). In multiple regression analyses comparing the reasons for physical abuse incidents (N = 826) with the nonabusive discipline incidents (N = 367), physical abuse was more frequently and statistically significantly associated with the child's refusing to do something, fighting or arguing with a sibling, playing with dangerous objects, creating some inconvenience (for example, bed wetting), lying or stealing, or being aggressive.

Such occurrences, while often exasperating, are not unusual in the course of childrearing. Since all parents must respond at one time or another to such child behavior and most do not physically abuse, it appears that the abusive parent's ability to cope effectively with frustrating or irritating situations is minimal.

Reasons for emotional abuse incidents (N = 189) were contrasted with those for nonabusive incidents of discipline. Marital conflict and adult anger occurred more often and statistically significantly with emotional abuse. Rather than the child's behavior eliciting the emotional abuse, anger and frustration associated with adult interpersonal relations appear to spill over on the child. The emotional abuse of the child reflects, once again, inadequate coping with difficult circumstances, in this case marital disagreements, on the part of the adults.

We compared the reasons for the occurrence of neglect (N = 802) to the reasons for physical abuse incidents, since comparison with nonabusive incidents of discipline did not seem appropriate. Neglect was found to be more frequently associated with the adult's refusal to meet family needs, the adult's providing inadequate supervision of children, excessive stress on adults, an unsafe home environment, the adult's lack of knowledge of child development, or an adult's physical or mental illness. While the crisis in this instance is that of meeting the demands of everyday living, again the difficulty can be attributed to the adult's inadequate skills for coping with such important yet mundane family crises.

These results suggest that each of the types of maltreatment occur under possibly difficult, but not unusual, circumstances in families with children. The circumstances under which physical abuse is most likely to occur are also the situations with opportunities for children to learn to cope with sibling rivalry and to develop independence, impulse control, and interpersonal trust. When physical abuse interferes with such exploration, the future development of self-control in these areas may be handicapped.

The finding that emotional abuse is associated with conflict between parents suggests that under these circumstances the maltreated child learns that the innocent bystander can be swept up and victimized in the conflict of others and that violent solutions to tension are chosen by adults.

In the case of neglect, the failure by adult family members to cope with the demands created by the needs of the children both deprives the children of basic necessities and models altogether inadequate or inappropriate ways to meet responsibilities for others.

Deficiency of Approval. High-quality parenting is clearly a complex and subtle combination of behaviors, involving responsibility for a child's physical survival and growth, intellectual and emotional development, and assimilation of cultural mores such that the child may emerge from the family setting prepared to live an independent, productive adult life in society. Not only nurturance of inborn capacities is required, but also "positive molding forces" which direct and guide the child's development (see, for example, Lidz, 1970).

Preliminary results of analyses of a small number of parent-child-inter-actions (N = 80) indicate that at least in the mother-child pairs studied, there is less parental approval behavior in the maltreatment group than in the comparison groups (Head Start, daycare, and protective service). In addition, a lower level of parental approval of the child was found to be associated with a greater degree of parental detachment from the child as rated by the observers ($r = -.47$, $p < .01$). Similar findings have been reported in another observational study of abusive and neglecting families (Burgess and Conger, 1978) which found that these families exhibited fewer positive and more negative interactions with each other than did control families, as well as lower base rates of interaction between parent and child. Children of abusive parents appear to be less likely than those of nonabusive parents to be guided in their development by "positive molding forces" within the family context.

Consequences of Maltreatment

In studies of maltreating families, the emphasis has generally been on the history and characteristics of the parents. More recent studies have shifted the focus to the children and the consequences of maltreatment on their development.

Lasting results of the physical injury itself in the form of scars, impaired motor coordination, or retardation, are serious consequences with many negative developmental implications for certain victims of child maltreatment. In our population, this is probably the case for, at most, 25.0 percent of the maltreated children.

In addition, the clinical literature has directed attention to a variety of potential long-term effects on development of victims of child maltreatment, including rejection of caretakers, diminished enjoyment of life, and cognitive deficits (Martin and Beezeley, 1976).

Foster Care. A powerful influence on the development of the maltreated child is the manner in which society has frequently intervened in the family in order to protect the child, or the way the family itself has responded to crises, namely, placing the child in a living situation outside the family.

Of 1118 children of families in the follow-up study, 62.0 percent of the 588 who were at some time victims of physical, emotional, or sexual abuse or gross neglect were at some point in their lives placed in a living situation outside the home, and 27.0 percent of their nonmaltreated siblings experienced placement outside the homes (Herrenkohl and Herrenkohl, 1979b). Thirteen percent of the maltreated children in the follow-up study had been placed outside the home even before the first documented maltreatment incident in their lives. These early placements occurred for a variety of reasons, including the family's loss of housing due to eviction or fire, or breakup of the parents with no one being able to function as a caretaker. One is immediately led to question the impact of these early separations of children from their parents on the attachment bonds between them, and to wonder whether weakening of such bonds might have occurred, thereby increasing the risk of subsequent maltreatment.

Fifty-nine percent of the maltreated children were placed at some time after the maltreatment incident. Thirty-nine percent of the children from these families who were ever placed outside the home were placed specifically for the purpose of protection from maltreatment. At the time of coding, 99 (40.0 percent) of the maltreated and placed children had not been returned. Of the 248 maltreated children who were placed after any of the four types of maltreatment and returned, 108 were maltreated again in some manner after their return although these were not necessarily incidents resulting in citation. These 108 children represent 44.0 percent of the maltreated children who were placed after being maltreated and were returned home sometime in the following months or years. Similarly, 43.0 percent of the children placed specifically for protection from maltreatment experienced a maltreatment episode after return.

One of the commonly discussed concerns about placement of children is the fact that children so often get caught in a depressing succession of moves once in the foster placement circuit (Wald, 1976). In this population, 34.0 percent of the maltreated children who were ever placed had three or more moves in their lives either from home to foster care, or foster home to foster home. These figures are comparable to those based on a study of statewide California data (Knitzer and Allen, 1978) which found that almost 30.0 percent of children placed by the child welfare system had been moved three or more times. Another survey of foster care studies (Wald, 1976) estimates that 50.0 percent of all foster children experience more than one placement, with at least 20.0 percent experiencing three or more placements.

In the follow-up study, the greater the total number of maltreatment incidents of any type experienced by a child, the more moves made by that child, both for protection from maltreatment and for other reasons ($r = .42$, $p = .001$). It is also the case that the more maltreatment experiences, the more hospitalization the child also tends to experience ($r = .14$, $p = .001$), this constituting another type of environmental shift. The maltreated child is thus exposed not only to the insecurity aroused by damaging or insufficient care at home, but also the trauma of continuing instability of home environment.

An early developmental task involves learning to trust others (Erikson, 1950). Goldstein, Freud, and Solnit (1973) warn that given the inherent impermanence of the foster care arrangement and the restrictions on the caretakers' powers, the child-foster parent relationship is subject to at least two dangers: the tendency on both sides to avoid deep emotional involvement in order to avoid suffering at separation, or the pain and confusion engendered by deep emotional involvement which is endangered because it is not recognized legally as a permanent bond.

In addition, the promotion of intellectual curiosity, achievements and personality integration are supported by secure attachment to a caretaker (Goldstein, Freud, and Solnit, 1973; Main, 1973; Sroufe, 1979), as is the ability to relate well to peers (Lieberman, 1977; Waters, Wippman, and Sroufe, 1979). Evidence is available that multiple placements negatively affect cognitive abilities and exploratory behavior of children (Wald, 1976). Thus, foster placement and the accompanying risk of disruptions in attachment in early childhood may have far-reaching effects on cognitive, social, and emotional development of the child.

The data from the follow-up study add to the concerns about the consequences of foster care as a protective measure for maltreated children. Physical safety and well-being do not appear to have been safeguarded in the long-run for almost half of the children who are returned to their parents from foster care. Many factors may be responsible including insufficient service to the family while the child is in foster care as well as damaging effects on the parent-child relationship of the separation trauma.

These results suggest a number of prescriptions: (1) the need to look upon foster placement as a last resort after all other efforts to provide support to the children while remaining in the family have failed or removal of the child is absolutely necessary to safeguard life or health, (2) the need to limit the time in which a child is allowed to remain in the impermanent status of foster care (such efforts are reflected in the recent California legislation), and (3) the need to support frequent visits between the child and the natural family, as long as return of the child to that family is planned. Goldstein, Freud, and Solnit (1973) refer to the need to keep alive in children's minds attachments to the family to which they will be ultimately returned. There is likewise a need to keep the family's attachment to the child alive. Similar points have been made in suggested guidelines for state intervention on behalf of neglected children (Wald, 1976).

The longitudinal study will explore the cognitive, social, and emotional status of children who have experienced foster care with that of children who have never been separated from their families.

Preschool Observations. Past research on normal child development has found a positive relationship between parental reliance on physical punishment and aggressiveness by the child (Bandura and Walters, 1963; Patterson, 1976; Sears, Maccoby, and Levin, 1957). In more recent research (George and Main, 1979; Reidy, 1977), physically abused children have been observed to display more aggressive behavior in free play with peers than nonabused children.

Observations of the preschool-age children in the coping study (Herrenkohl and Herrenkohl, in preparation), have extended the findings cited above of increased aggression among physically abused infants (George and Main, 1979) and school-age children (Reidy, 1977) to the three- to five-year-old age range. Our measure of aggression was the group of items which emerged as the first factor in a factor analysis of the 151 ratings made by observers on the basis of two half-hour observations, one week apart, of free play with peers. In these data, aggression was found to be associated with low frustration tolerance such that an aggressive response to difficult tasks or interfering behavior by others was significantly more likely ($p < .05$) among maltreated than nonmaltreated children. These findings are the results of regression analyses which controlled for variations in family characteristics (for example, SES, single vs. two-parent households, and mother's level of education), classroom characteristics (for example, encouragement of social interaction and emphasis on rules), and child-related characteristics (for example, length of time in classroom, age, and sex).

There may be a number of contributing factors underlying this finding. One is modelling as suggested above. Children who have been exposed to maltreating behavior by adults (either toward themselves or toward other family members) have seen their parents respond to stressful pressures by exploding and venting their anger physically on others and have learned this pattern of response to frustration.

Secondly, maltreated children have frequently been described as "hypervigilant" (Martin and Beezely, 1976, 1980). They appear to be constantly on the alert for possible danger, scanning the environment for signs of impending attack. Such children may be quick to interpret any interruption or obstacle as such a danger signal and thus respond aggressively because they interpret frustrating circumstances as a threat to physical survival.

As discussed earlier, children from maltreating families may have been exposed to more frustrating circumstances at home — their activities often interrupted by caretakers who, feeling stressed themselves, cannot tolerate the noise and activity level of an active preschooler. Such children might, then, respond more negatively to any additional frustrations in the classroom, their tolerance level being lower because of the extent of restrictions they have previously experienced at home.

These data dramatize the potential for interaction of systems at different levels of the ecological model in the consequences of maltreatment: children raised in the maltreating environment of the family microsystem may, as adults, contribute to their isolation from support systems at the macrosystem level by virtue of the developmental deficits they exhibit when interacting with peers even as youngsters. Studies of the skills involved in the ability to develop friendships among nursery-school-age children (Rubin, 1980) have pointed to the importance of successful conflict-resolution as a central issue, even in the three- to five-year-old age range. The greater tendency among maltreated children as a group to exhibit aggressive responses to all frustrations, both object- and people-related, would suggest that many maltreated children may well be exhibiting the beginnings of a pattern at three and four years of age which will make social isolation more likely as a child and as an adult.

Conclusions

The preceding has reviewed some antecedents of maltreatment (that is, conditions that increase its likelihood), qualities of the parent-child interaction (that is, the context in which maltreatment occurs), and some consequences of maltreatment (that is, immediate and longer-term effects on the child's development). The results reported above involved statistically significant but, for the most part, relatively modest associations between antecedents and the occurrence of maltreatment. While such small relationships may signify that the one or two major determinants have yet to be assessed empirically, we think it is more likely that such findings reflect the multidetermined nature of conditions associated with each of the types of maltreatment. Thus, one would expect a large number of relatively small relationships.

We view an ecological model of child maltreatment to be the most meaningful approach to integrating the complexity of data and theory. The ecological context of maltreatment might be thought of as a set of everwidening circles. At the center is the parent-child interaction where the child learns social and coping skills and develops a sense of self-worth and social competence. These interactions are set within a family network of social relationships which expose the child to a variety of models of interpersonal and communication skills. The satisfactions or dissatisfactions of these relationships also reverberate in the parent-child relationship. In a still wider context, the family is set within a neighborhood which reflects for the child and parent the broader community and cultural expectations for behavior. Furthermore, the neighborhood affects and is affected by the quality of family life.

One version of the model (Garbarino, 1977) poses two "necessary" conditions for the occurrence of child maltreatment: cultural support legitimizing the use of force against children at the level of macrosystems and isolation from potential support systems (the mesosystems of neighborhood, social services, politics, and the economy). Sufficient conditions include the effects of stress on the family system, feelings of helplessness on the part of caretakers confronting disruptive forces within or outside the family, and limited experience of the caregiver in the practice of caretaker role functions.

The research results described above also suggest that the maltreating family may be a context in which problem solving as a general coping skill is inadequately modelled or encouraged. Instead, frustration tolerance of the parents may be low, conflict high, and explosive solutions frequent. While the antecedents of maltreatment may influence susceptibility to maltreating, they do not explain the act or succession of acts. Rather, each type of maltreatment is the result of an inadequate attempt to cope with aspects of everyday family life that the individual perceives as threatening because of the awareness that the skill and resources necessary to master difficulties are lacking.

Children developing in such a context may experience a variety of effects due to the maltreatment itself or the maltreating family environment: (1) physical damage resulting from neglect or abuse (2) the frustration of activities that are an important part of developing self-control and frustration tolerance; and (3) the lack of nurturance and guidance attendant on positive reinforcement of activities that are approved by the parent. Further, many may suffer the consequences of an unstable home environment and disruptions in early attachments that limit the likelihood of successful achievement of such early and basic developmental tasks as learning to trust others. As a result, the degree of social competence that is necessary for adequate functioning as a parent and in society at large may not develop. One long-range result is that as an adult the maltreating cycle may be repeated.

The emphasis in this chapter has been on the potentially devastating effects of the maltreatment context. However, just as not all families under stress are maltreating, not all children who are maltreated appear to manifest such consequences of maltreatment. The conditions in the context or the qualities of the child that serve as protection from maltreatment are unclear. There may be other factors in the environment not yet considered in the analyses, such as a supportive, nurturant relative or other significant adult, or a high level of intellectual ability in the child. Future analyses of these data may provide greater insight into the process by which the development of coping skills is thwarted among some maltreatment victims, as well as the conditions which allow some children to emerge relatively unscathed from similar environments.

References

Achenbach, T. M. "The Child Behavior Profile." Part One: "Boys Ages 6–11." *Journal of Consulting and Clinical Psychology,* 1978, *46*(3), 478–488.

Achenbach, T. M., and Edelbrock, C. "The Child Behavior Profile." Part Two: "Boys Aged 12–16 and Girls Aged 6–11 and 12–16." *Journal of Consulting and Clinical Psychology,* 1979, *47*(2), 223–233.

Bandura, A., and Walters, R. H. *Social Learning and Personality Development.* New York: Holt, 1963.

Belsky, J. "Child Maltreatment: An Ecological Integration." *American Psychologist,* 1980, *35,* 320–335.

Brazelton, T. B. *Neonatal Behavioral Assessment Scale.* National Spastics Society Monograph. London: Heineman, 1973.

74

Bronfenbrenner, U. "Toward an Experimental Ecology of Human Development." *American Psychologist,* 1977, *32*(7), 513-531.

Burgess, R., and Conger, R. "Family Interaction in Abusive, Neglectful, and Normal Families." *Child Development,* 1978, *49,* 1163-1173.

Egeland, B., and Brunnquell, D. "An At-Risk Approach to the Study of Child Abuse: Some Preliminary Findings." *Journal of the American Academy of Child Psychiatry,* 1979, *18*(2), 219-235.

Egeland, B., Breitenbucher, M., and Rosenberg, D. "Prospective Study of the Significance of Life Stress in the Etiology of Child Abuse." *Journal of Consulting and Clinical Psychology,* 1980, *48*(2), 195-205.

Emmerich, W. *Disadvantaged Children and Their First School Experiences.* Princeton, N.J.: Educational Testing Service, 1971.

Erikson, E. H. *Childhood and Society.* New York: Norton, 1950.

Friedrich, W. W., and Boriskin, J. A. "The Role of the Child in Abuse." *American Journal of Orthopsychiatry,* 1976, *40,* 580-590.

Furstenberg, F. F., Jr. "Premarital Pregnancy and Marital Instability." *Journal of Social Issues,* 1976, *32*(1), 67-86.

Garbarino, J. "The Human Ecology of Child Maltreatment: A Conceptual Model for Research." *Journal of Marriage and the Family,* 1977, *39,* 721-735.

Garbarino, J., and Stocking, S. H. *Protecting Children from Abuse and Neglect.* San Francisco: Jossey-Bass, 1980.

Gelles, R. "Child Abuse as Psychopathology: A Sociological Critique and Reformulation." *American Journal of Orthopsychiatry,* 1973, *43,* 611-621.

George, C., and Main, M. "Social Interactions of Young Abused Children: Approach, Avoidance, and Aggression." *Child Development,* 1979, *50,* 306-318.

Gil, D. *Violence Against Children.* Cambridge, Mass.: Harvard University Press, 1970.

Giovannoni, J., and Becerra, R. M. *Defining Child Abuse.* New York: Free Press, 1979.

Goldstein, J., Freud, A., and Solnit, A. J. *Beyond the Best Interests of the Child.* New York: Free Press, 1973.

Herrenkohl, E. C., and Herrenkohl, R. C., "A Comparison of Abused Children and their Nonabused Siblings." *Journal of the American Academy of Child Psychiatry,* 1979a, *18*(2), 260-269.

Herrenkohl, E. C., and Herrenkohl, R. C. "Foster Care of Abused Children: What Happens After Placement?" Paper presented the National Conference on Child Abuse and Neglect in Los Angeles, California, October 1979b.

Herrenkohl, E. C. and Herrenkohl, R. C. "Classroom Observations of Abused and Non-Abused Preschool Children." In preparation.

Herrenkohl, R. C., Herrenkohl, E. C., and Egolf, B. "Circumstances Surrounding the Occurrence of Child Abuse." In preparation.

Herrenkohl, R. C., Herrenkohl, E. C., Egolf, B., and Seech, M. "The Repetition of Child Abuse: How Frequently Does It Occur?" *International Journal of Child Abuse and Neglect,* 1979, *3*(1), 67-72.

Hetherington, E. M., and Parke, R. D. *Child Psychology, A Contemporary Viewpoint.* (2nd ed.) New York: McGraw-Hill, 1979.

Justice, B., and Justice, R. *The Abusing Family.* New York: Human Sciences Press, 1976.

Kempe, R. S., and Kempe, C. H. *Child Abuse.* Cambridge, Mass.: Harvard University Press, 1978.

Knitzer, J., and Allen, M. J. *Children Without Homes.* Washington, D.C.: Children's Defense Fund, 1978.

Lieberman, A. F. "Preschoolers' Competence with a Peer: Relations with Attachment and Peer Experience." *Child Development,* 1977, *48,* 1277-1287.

Lidz, T. "The Family as the Developmental Setting." In E. J. Anthony and C. Kouper-nik (Eds.), *The Child in His Family*. Vol. 1. New York: Wiley, 1970.

Main, M. "Exploration, Play, and Level of Cognitive Functioning as Related to Child-Mother Attachment." Unpublished doctoral dissertation, Johns Hopkins University, 1973.

Martin, H. "Which Children Get Abused." In H. Martin (Ed.), *The Abused Child*. Cambridge, Mass.: Ballinger, 1976.

Martin, H., and Beezeley, P. "Personality of Abused Children." In H. Martin (Ed.), *The Abused Child*. Cambridge, Mass.: Ballinger, 1976.

Martin, H., and Beezeley, P. "Behavioral Observations of Abused Children." In J. V. Cook and R. T. Bowles (Eds.), *Child Abuse: Commission and Omission*. Toronto, Canada: Butterworth, 1980.

Parke, R. D. "Socialization into Child Abuse." In J. V. Cook and R. T. Bowles (Eds.), *Child Abuse: Commission and Omission*. Toronto, Canada: Butterworth, 1980.

Parke, R. D., and Collmer, C. "Child Abuse: An Interdisciplinary Analysis." In E. M. Hetherington (Ed.), *Review of Child Development Research*. Vol. 5. Chicago: University of Chicago Press, 1975.

Patterson, J. R. "The Aggressive Child: Victim and Architect of a Coercial System." In E. J. Mash, L. A. Hamerlynck, and L. C. Handy (Eds.), *Behavior Modification and Families*. New York: Brunner/Mazel, 1976.

Polansky, N. A., Borgman, R. D., and De Saix, C. *Roots of Futility*. San Francisco: Jossey-Bass, 1972.

Reidy, T. J. "The Aggressive Characteristics of Abused and Neglected Children." *Journal of Clinical Psychology*, 1977, *33*(4), 1140–1145.

Rosenzweig, S. *The Rosenzweig Picture Frustration Study, Basic Manual*. St. Louis, Mo.: Rana House, 1978.

Roskies, E., and Lazarus, R. S. "Coping Theory and the Teaching of Coping Skills." In P. O. Davidson and S. M. Davidson (Eds.), *Behavioral Medicine: Changing Life-styles*. New York: Brunner/Mazel, 1980.

Rubin, Z. *Children's Friendships*. Cambridge, Mass.: Harvard University Press, 1980.

Russell, C. S. "Unscheduled Parenthood: Transition to 'Parent' for the Teenager." *Journal of Social Issues*, 1980, *36*(1), 45–63.

Sears, R. R., Maccoby, E., and Levin, H. *Patterns of Child Rearing*. Evanston, Ill.: Row, Peterson, 1957.

Simkins, C. G., and others. *Child Abuse and Neglect in Families: An Analysis of Family-Focused Projects on Child Abuse and Neglect*. Funded by HEW's Administration on Children, Youth, and Families, Center for Comm. Studies, George Peabody Company, 1979.

Smith, S. "The Battered Child Syndrome." *Psychiatric Journal of the University of Ottawa*, 1976, *1*, 158–164.

Steele, B., and Pollock, C. "A Psychiatric Study of Parents Who Abuse Infants and Small Children," In R. E. Helfer and C. H. Kempe (Eds.), *The Battered Child*. (2nd ed.) Chicago: Unversity of Chicago Press, 1974.

Straus, M., Gelles, R. J., and Steinmetz, S. K. *Behind Closed Doors: Violence in the American Family*. New York: Anchor Press, Doubleday, 1980.

Thompson, E. M., and others. *Child Abuse: A Community Challenge*. East Aurora, N. Y.: Henry Steward, 1971.

Sroufe, L. A. "The Coherence of Individual Development." *American Pschyologist*, 1979, *34*(10), 834–841.

Wald, M. "State Intervention on Behalf of 'Neglected' Children: Standards for Removal of Children from Their Homes, Monitoring the Status of Children in Foster Care, and Termination of Parental Rights." *Stanford Law Review*, 1976, *28*, 623–707.

Waters, E., Wippman, J., and Sroufe, L. A. "Attachment, Positive Affect, and Competence in the Peer Group: Two Studies in Construct Validation." *Child Development,* 1979, *50,* 821–829.

Zigler, E., and Trickett, P. K. "IQ, Social Competence, and Evaluation of Early Childhood Intervention Programs." *American Psychologist,* 1978, *33,* 780–798.

Roy C. Herrenkohl is professor of social psychology and director, Center for Social Research, Lehigh University.

Ellen C. Herrenkohl is a research scientist in the Lehigh University Center for Social Research. She is also in the private practice of clinical psychology.

Three patterns of maltreatment in addition to physical abuse were identified
as part of a prospective study of the antecedents of child maltreatment.
Over the first two years of the infants' life, these different forms of
maltreatment were found to have cumulative and differential negative
effects upon development.

Developmental Sequelae of Maltreatment in Infancy

Byron Egeland
Alan Sroufe

In the area of socioemotional development, even the obvious is often difficult
to demonstrate (for example, the existence of attachment, the stability of personality, the influence of family systems). Uncovering the developmental consequences of child abuse is a prime example. Much of the research in this area
has focused on intellectual development, and even in that domain, the effects
of abuse have been difficult to separate from the effects of social class (Elmer,
1977). Yet, no one can doubt that there are consequences to being physically
abused.

In this chapter we present data from a prospective, longitudinal investigation of early development. The results provide substantial documentation
of the negative effects of physical abuse, apart from the consequences of class
membership, and also illustrate the malignancy of other forms of maltreatment. By selecting a range of outcome measures and using a prospective

The first three years of this project were supported by a grant from the National
Center on Child Abuse and Neglect, Administration for Children, Youth, and Fami-
lies, Office of Human Development. The project is currently supported by a grant from
Maternal and Child Health and Crippled Children's Services.

design, we hoped to avoid some of the problems and complexities of earlier investigations, particularly those studies without control groups.

First, our study was focused on an urban poor population in which young, relatively uneducated mothers were heavily represented. Children who have been maltreated often are raised in environments that hinder development, such as overcrowded home situations that lack the stimulation and encouragement necessary for normal development. The parent-child relationships of maltreating families are characterized by a number of negative qualities that are associated with harsh treatment and a lack of positive qualities such as praise and encouragement, which are essential for the optimal development of the child (Burgess and Conger, 1977; Herrenkohl and Herrenkohl, 1979). All of these factors, in addition to physical abuse, were expected to be extensive in our sample, making it possible to separate the effects of maltreatment and other negative environmental influences from the effects of physical abuse alone.

Second, virtually every study of abuse has pointed to a diversity of outcomes. The percentage of abused children who are of below average intelligence varies among studies (Martin, 1972; Morse, Sahler, and Friedman, 1970; Sandgrund, Gaines, and Green, 1974), and the range of IQs within particular studies is wide. Martin, Beezeley, Conway, and Kempe (1974) reported the mean IQ for their group to be 92.3, with a standard deviation of 21.8 and a range from 15.0 to 131.0.

The social/emotional consequences of abuse are also highly varied. Ounsted, Oppenheimer, and Lindsay (1974) described the abused child as silent, passive, and underachieving, but perceptive and sensitive to what is going on in the environment. They call the extreme form of this pattern "frozen watchfulness." Other investigators have described abused children as unable to relax and enjoy themselves (Martin and Beezeley, 1977) and having low self-esteem and displaying behaviors that made peers, parents, and teachers reject them (Martin and Beezeley, 1977). Many abused children are described as withdrawn, extremely passive, apathetic, and totally unresponsive to others, particularly the mother (Galdston, 1965; Martin and Beezeley, 1977; Terr, 1970); whereas others are called aggressive, hostile, negative, and oppositional (Martin and Beezeley, 1977; Terr, 1970). A similar diversity of outcome is reported by Kempe and Kempe (1978), whose sample of abused children is one of the largest. The children's characteristics included compliance and acceptance of whatever happened, hyperactivity, aggressiveness, lack of identity, impaired social relations, and lack of trust.

Elmer (1977), who systematically controlled for SES and hospitalization, found tremendous variation in scores within the abuse group on every variable, and she concluded that, "Factors other than abuse might account for the observed variation among the individual children" (p. 77). Elmer found few group differences across a variety of measures; however, she found a large number of problems and deficiencies for children in all three groups. She concluded that membership in the lower social class was an underlying factor contributing to these widespread difficulties and stated, "The results of child abuse are less potent for the child's development than class membership" (p. 110).

Such diversity of outcome was anticipated in our research by building in a range of developmentally salient outcome measures. Analyses were carried out at different levels, from molecular to more molar behavior, and procedures were evolved to summarize findings across several areas of functioning.

Third, in our study we sought to place physical abuse in the larger context of the caretaking environment. An abusive situation in which there is frequent, severe physical punishment and ongoing hostility might well lead to different developmental outcomes than a situation where the parent is relatively passive but has occasional violent outbursts. Previous investigators have not attempted to clearly define subgroups of abuse and maltreatment within the context of the broader caretaking environment in which the child is raised. Some abused children are also physically and emotionally neglected, while others are rejected, abandoned, or cared for in a highly inconsistent fashion. Each setting may differentially affect the child's development. The consequences of abuse are mediated by a variety of factors, including caretaker characteristics, environmental circumstances, life stress, and support from family, friends, and community, as well as the child's temperament and past developmental history.

Fourth, our study was prospective and began before the birth of the child. Though difficult, there are a number of advantages of such a strategy (see Egeland and Brunnquell, 1979). For this particular investigation, there are two major advantages: (1) It permits collection of early data on subjects who later drop out. High drop-out rates, which have plagued past studies (see, for example, Elmer, 1977), may make significant group differences difficult to obtain if drop outs from the abuse group have more negative outcomes. (2) It allows some disentangling of child and parenting factors. While most investigators suggest multifactor models of childhood problems (Cicchetti, Taraldson, and Egeland, 1978; Egeland, Cicchetti, and Taraldson, 1976; Parke and Collmer, 1975; Sameroff and Chandler, 1975), some have even gone so far as to suggest that certain characteristics (for example, aggression, hyperactivity) of the children themselves play a major part in causing the maltreatment (Terr, 1970). Our data allow examination of the child (and parent) both before and after maltreatment has begun.

Finally, we were concerned about the outcome variables and the procedures used to assess them. To understand the consequences of maltreatment fully, researchers cannot be content with simple isomorphic outcome variables such as aggression, nor can they expect to find a direct linear relationship between maltreatment and specific outcomes. The effects of maltreatment are most likely cumulative, so it is important that assessments be done longitudinally, using measures that are keyed to the relevant developmental issues of each age period (see Cicchetti and Rizley, this volume). Even though the consequences of maltreatment are complex, they are not beyond comprehension. Predictable ties between specific outcomes and antecedents can be established. However, it is clear that researchers need to know a great deal about the overall environment and context of the abuse and use a range of differentiated outcome measures. Given certain relationships, caretaking histories, and circumstances, maltreatment may tend to lead to particular outcomes. With different histories or circumstances, different classes of outcome may result. The remainder of this chapter is a report of an investigation of the relation between different forms of maltreatment and developmental outcomes during the first two years of the infant's life. This prospective, longitudinal study was designed with the methodological concerns just discussed as guides.

The Minnesota Mother-Child Project

For five years we have been involved in a multivariate prospective study of children at risk for abuse, neglect, and poor developmental outcome — first with funding from the National Center on Child Abuse and Neglect (Egeland and Deinard, 1975b) and subsequently with a grant from Maternal and Child Health (Egeland, Deinard, and Sroufe, 1977). Beginning with the third trimester of pregnancy, 200 families (originally 267) have been followed in some detail. We have obtained data on parent personality, attitudes, expectations, views on child development, and understanding of children; newborn status, behavior, and "temperament" (in the hospital and at home); early mother-infant interaction, later interaction, attachment, parental control, and discipline techniques; toddler and preschool play, exploration, and problem solving (Brunnquell, Crichton, and Egeland, in press; Egeland, Breitenbucher, and Rosenberg, 1980; Egeland and Brunnquell, 1979). Except for the personality data, most of this data is derived from direct observation, usually using procedures extensively validated prior to this research. In addition, regular interviews have been used to obtain information on life stress and circumstances, including mother's relationships, her view of her child, and her family history. It has not been possible to include fathers. Sixty-two percent of the mothers were unwed at the time of their infant's birth and for many who were in relationships, the relationship was unstable.

Our sample was selected not because maltreatment had been detected, but because these families were viewed at risk for developmental problems, due to the youth of the mothers (40.0 percent were teenagers), their poverty and limited education, and, in general, their limited resources and caretaking skills. Given the characteristics of our sample, it is possible to describe more than one kind of maltreatment. It is also possible to compare outcomes of maltreatment cases with other cases where the circumstances usually associated with maltreatment are present but maltreatment does not occur. The nonmaltreated children from the sample serve as controls, which allows us to distinguish consequences of maltreatment from those of poverty and membership in a low SES group.

In general, it is our objective to provide an extended and differentiated definition of maltreatment as well as a more elaborated conception of outcome. From a researcher's point of view, forms of maltreatment other than obvious physical abuse must be defined to help uncover the particular consequences of physical abuse and distinguish them from the consequences of physical abuse in interaction with other forms of inadequate care. In this chapter we report the effects of physical abuse on various child outcome measures during the first two years of the infant's life. In addition, we report the effects on the child's development of three different forms or patterns of maltreatment. Specifically, we attempt to determine the consequences of each form of maltreatment with and without physical abuse. Our range of outcome measures — mother-infant interaction, attachment, play, and problem solving — allows discovery of the arenas in which negative consequences appear as well as their form.

In addition to physical abuse, three maltreatment groups were selected: hostile/verbally abusive, psychologically unavailable, and neglectful. The behaviors of mothers in the physical abuse group ranged from frequent and intense spanking in disciplining their children to unprovoked angry outbursts resulting in such injuries as severe cigarette burns. The spankings were beyond what would normally be expected in disciplining a child. In all cases the abuse was seen as potentially physically damaging to the child; in many instances bruises and cuts were observed or more serious injuries were reported in hospital and public health clinic files. Many of these mothers can be described as highly rejecting of their children, while others are less rejecting and more prone to violent, unprovoked outbursts.

The mothers in the hostile group were chronically verbally abusive toward their children. They constantly found fault with their children and criticized them in an extremely harsh fashion. These mothers differ from those in the physical abuse group in the chronic nature of their hostility and their constant harrassment of their children. In virtually every situation where mothers in the hostile group interacted with their children, there was constant berating and harrassment. In contrast, mothers who physically abused their children were not overtly hostile to or constantly rejecting of their children. Despite these differences, there is a considerable overlap between the physical abuse and hostile groups.

The mothers in the psychologically unavailable group were character-ized by a lack of responsiveness to their children and, in many instances, a passive rejection of them. These mothers were detached and emotionally unin-volved while interacting with their children and displayed little interest in them. In general, they were withdrawn, appeared depressed, and displayed flat affect. There was virtually no indication of any pleasure, gratification, or satisfaction derived from their relationship with their children. The mother interacted with the child only when it was necessary, and when she did inter-act, it was obvious that a real effort was required.

The mothers in the neglect group have been identified as not providing proper care and, to some extent, they were irresponsible or incompetent in managing the day-to-day child care activities. These mothers often did not provide for the necessary health or physical care of the children, nor did they protect them from possible dangerous situations in the home. In general, the children in this group experienced very bad living conditions. At times, these mothers appeared interested in the well-being of their children, but they did not have the caretaking skill, knowledge, or understanding to provide ade-quate care on a consistent basis. They appeared totally irresponsible in caring for their infants, and, in many instances, they were irresponsible in managing their own lives.

The mothers in the maltreatment groups were selected on the basis of information obtained from observations of the mother and infant in the home at seven and ten days and at three, six (two visits), and twelve months. During each of these visits, a Child Care Rating Scale was completed (Egeland and Deinard, 1975a), and the mother was asked questions regarding her care-taking skills, feelings toward the infant, disciplinary practices, and so on. The decisions were primarily based on these sources of information and particu-larly each staff member's knowledge of the mother. In addition, observational data and other information were systematically collected when each mother visited the Maternal and Infant Care Clinic. Data were also collected at the nine, twelve, eighteen, and twenty-four month visits to our laboratory. Infor-mation from the case records of the county hospital, Maternal and Infant Care Clinics, and welfare agency was also considered in selecting mothers from our high-risk sample for placement in one of the four maltreatment groups. This additional information was used to support the selections.

The validity of these decisions is supported by various facts. All the mothers in the physical abuse group are or have been under the care of child protection or have been referred to child protection by someone outside of our project. The mothers in the neglect group currently are or have been under the care and protection of a public health nurse or child protection. Indepen-dent raters' observations of the mother and infant at twelve and eighteen months in a situation requiring limit setting for the child and at twenty-four months in a problem-solving task support the selection of mothers in the psychologically unavailable and hostile groups.

A control group of mothers who provided adequate care was selected from the remaining sample. If there was some question whether a mother was maltreating a child or if the maltreatment was borderline, the case was not included in the control group or any of the maltreatment groups. Of approximately 200 cases considered from the total at-risk sample on whom data were available the first two years, twenty-four mothers were in the physical abuse group, nineteen in the hostile group, nineteen in the psychologically unavailable group, twenty-five neglected their children, and eighty-five were in the control group. Of the nineteen hostile mothers, fifteen were also in the physical abuse group. Unfortunately for purposes of statistical analysis, this results in an $N = 4$ for the hostile without physical abuse group. Of the nineteen mothers in the psychologically unavailable group, twelve out of nineteen were in the physical abuse group, and thirteen of twenty-four mothers in the neglect group also physically abused their children.

In the analyses reported here, the developmental consequences of maltreatment and inappropriate caretaking were examined over the first two years of the infant's life. The assessments at three, six, twelve, eighteen, and twenty-four months were designed to measure the child's competence in the salient developmental tasks at that particular age period. The Bayley Scales of Infant Development (BSID) were administered at nine and twelve months in order to have an overall index of cognitive development. At three months after birth, the mother and infant were observed in a feeding situation, and at six months mother and infant were observed in two feeding and one play situation (Vaughn, Taraldson, Crichton, and Egeland, 1980). After observing the feeding and play sessions, the observer rated a variety of mother, infant, and interactional behaviors. Separate factor analyses of the feeding and play situations resulted in a three-factor solution, and in each case one of the factors was a baby factor. The three- and six-month baby feeding factor loaded on the following items: baby's responsiveness to mother's interactions, social behavior of the baby, and baby's disposition. The items loading on the baby play factor were baby's activity level, baby's coordination, baby's satisfaction, and baby's attention.

Quality of attachment was assessed at twelve and eighteen months using Ainsworth, Blehar, Waters, and Wall's (1978) Strange Situation procedure. The procedure consists of eight brief separation and reunion episodes designed to highlight the operation of the attachment system. Individual differences in the use of mother as a secure base from which to explore and in the ability to be comforted by the mother's presence are scored primarily from episodes involving reunion with the mother. Securely attached infants (group B) explore actively in preseparation episodes; they actively greet or seek contact with the mother in reunion episodes and are able to return to exploration in mother's presence. There are two groups of anxiously attached infants. Anxious/avoidant infants (group A) tend to explore without interaction in preseparation episodes; they behave similarly toward mother and stranger, and upon reunion they actively avert gaze and ignore mother. Anxious/resistant infants (group C) are often distressed by the unfamiliar room and the unfamiliar adult, even in mother's presence. Their exploratory behavior is limited, and they are very distressed by separation. In reunion episodes they are often difficult to comfort and often show anger and active resistance to physical contact or interaction (Ainsworth, Blehar, Waters, and Wall, 1978). A fourth group, considered anxiously attached but neither avoidant nor resistant (for example, apathetic or disorganized) was included at eighteen months. Since these infants were not classifiable into one of the three Ainsworth categories, we classified them as Group D.

At twenty-four months the child's style and approach in a problem-solving situation were assessed. For the toddler, measures of emerging autonomy, independent environmental engagement, and resources to cope with a frustrating situation reflect the salient developmental task for this age. The tool-use situation is a laboratory procedure developed by Matas, Arend, and Sroufe (1978), consisting of four tool-using, problem-solving tasks. Mother is present in the room with the toddler and is told to let the child first work on the problem independently and then to "give any help you think the child needs." The first two problems were simple and were not included in the scoring. The third and fourth problems were increasingly difficult: putting two sticks together, end to end, in order to get a lure from a long tube, and weighting down the end of a lever with a block to raise candy through a hole in a plexiglas box. This latter problem cannot be solved by a two-year-old without the help of an adult. The procedure was videotaped, and a set of observers recorded the frequency of the following discrete behaviors: whining, aggressive behaviors, frustration, positive and negative affect, and noncompliance. At a more behavioral level, the following behaviors were rated by another set of observers on a five- to seven-point scale: enthusiasm, dependency, noncompliance, anger, frustration toward the mother, coping, and persistence. Coding of the mother and child variables were done by totally independent groups of coders. None of the coders had any knowledge of mother groups or life history information.

Results

In the first set of analyses, the total physical abuse group is compared with the control on each variable. This group consists of all the physically abusing mothers regardless of whether they were in other maltreatment groups. There were no significant differences between the two groups on the three-and six-month baby feeding, six-month play factor score, or the BSID, which was given at 9 months.

The proportions of infants in the physical abuse group classified as securely attached (Bs), anxious/avoidant (As), and anxious/resistant (Cs) at twelve and eighteen months were twenty-seven percent, fifty-five percent, and eighteen percent and thirty-three percent, and forty-eight percent, and nineteen percent respectively. The attachment classifications for the control group at twelve months were As = 18 percent, Bs = 67 percent, and Cs = 15 percent; at 18 months As = 16 percent, Bs = 71 percent, and Cs = 13 percent, which are approximately the same as typically found in middle class samples (Ainsworth and others, 1978; Waters, 1978). By eighteen months the comparison between abused and control children is statistically significant when the two anxiously attached groups are combined.

A number of differences were found between the physical abuse group and controls on the two-year problem-solving situation. The physical abuse group had significantly higher scores on the frequency of observed aggressive behaviors, frustration, noncompliance, and lower scores on positive affect. On Task 3, the physical abuse group showed significantly more whining and non-compliant behavior; but by Task 4 there was no difference between the two groups. There was no overall difference in the frequency of whining between the two groups.

On the more global ratings, the physical abuse group obtained a higher score on anger, frustration directed toward the mother, and noncompliance and a lower score on enthusiasm compared to the control group. There was no difference between the two groups on the BSID given at twenty-four months.

The next set of analyses examined the effects on the child's development of hostile, psychologically unavailable, and neglectful patterns of child-rearing with and without physical abuse. Specifically, we examined what effects these different forms of maltreatment or inappropriate childrearing have on the child's development and what effects physical abuse has when it is combined with another form of maltreatment. Twenty-two of the twenty-four children in the physical abuse group were also in other maltreatment groups; each of the maltreatment groups was broken down into subgroups depending on whether physical abuse was also present.

The first of these analyses involved comparing the verbally hostile but not physically abusive mothers with the group who were hostile and physically abusive. In turn, these two groups were compared to the control group. There were no differences in three- and six-month feeding and play, nine-month BSID, or twelve-month Strange Situation. At eighteen months, the groups differed statistically significantly in the proportion of securely and anxiously attached infants. The majority of infants who were in the hostile only group were classified as group D. The cumulative effects of physical abuse with a hostile pattern of childrearing can be noted by the fact that the majority of these infants were anxiously attached: As (15 percent), Cs (31 percent), or Ds (8 percent).

More frustration and anger was observed in the problem-solving task at twenty-four months in both the hostile only and hostile with physical abuse groups compared to the control group. Similar findings were obtained with the two-year global ratings. The hostile pattern of childrearing with and without physical abuse results in higher ratings of noncompliance and anger. The toddlers in the hostile without physical abuse group had a higher rating on frustration directed at the mother than the control group.

Differences between these two forms of maltreatment were found on the BSID at twenty-four months. The infants of hostile only mothers obtained an average DQ of 105, which was significantly higher than the average DQ of 90 for the toddlers of hostile mothers who were also physically abusive (control's average DQ = 107). In general, the hostile pattern of childrearing along with physical abuse had a negative effect on the toddler's development, shown particularly by high frustration, constant noncompliance, and anger. This pattern did not seem to be related to the emotional behaviors of enthusiasm and positive and negative affect; nor was it related to overall persistence or coping. Except for DQ, the negative effects of physical abuse along with a hostile pattern of childrearing were not significantly greater than a hostile pattern of childrearing alone. The findings from this set of analyses must be considered highly tentative, since there were only four subjects in the hostile without physical abuse group. Understandably, mothers who display a hostile style of caretaking are also physically abusive.

The next set of analyses involved the psychologically unavailable style of childrearing, with and without physical abuse. The infants in the psychologically unavailable without physical abuse group had a significantly higher three-month baby factor score compared to the control group, but by six months their scores had significantly declined to the point where there was no difference among the three groups. There were no differences among the groups on the BSID given at nine months.

Differences in the proportion of infants in the attachment groups for the control and psychologically unavailable with and without physical abuse groups approached significance at twelve months and were highly significant at eighteen months. Forty-three percent of the infants in the psychologically unavailable without physical abuse group were classified as As at twelve months; at eighteen months, 86 percent were As. There were no Cs in this group at twelve months and, surprisingly, at eighteen months there were *no* securely attached infants. According to these results, a mother who is emotionally unavailable is likely to have an infant with a specific attachment pattern — anxious/avoidant. The attachment pattern changes when physical abuse is combined with psychological unavailability. At twelve months there were more Cs and fewer Bs in the combined group; at eighteen months there were more Bs in the combined group than in the psychologically unavailable without physical abuse group.

The cumulative effects of chronic psychological unavailability are obvious in the changes in attachment classification that occur between twelve and eighteen months. At twelve months the majority of infants (57 percent) in the psychologically unavailable without physical abuse group were securely attached. By eighteen months none of the infants in this group was classified as securely attached; 14 percent were classified as group D and the remainder, 86 percent, were classified as As.

At twenty-four months, the negative effects of psychological unavailability were noted on most of the frequency counts and global ratings. The frequency of frustration, whining, and negative affect was greatest for the psychologically unavailable without physical abuse group, and they showed frustration and anger earlier in the problem-solving situation. The psychologically unavailable with physical abuse group was more likely to display these behaviors on the more difficult fourth problem. Both the psychologically unavailable groups displayed less positive affect than the control group. Of the global ratings, only enthusiasm differentiated the psychologically unavailable with and without physical abuse groups, with the latter being lower. Both of these groups were rated higher on noncompliance, anger, and frustration directed at the mother than the control group.

Both of these groups had lower BSID DQs at twenty-four months than the control group. What is particularly interesting is the decline between nine and twenty-four months. At nine months the average mental score for the psychologically unavailable without physical abuse group was 118, and for the psychologically unavailable with physical abuse group it was 121. By twenty-four months the DQs were 87 and 83, respectively. All groups showed a decline, but this was the largest.

Comparing the controls and the neglecting with and without physical abuse groups, there were no differences on the three- and six-months baby factor scores or the nine-month BSID mental and motor scores. There were striking differences in attachment classifications at twelve months. The neglect with and without physical abuse groups had 27 percent and 29 percent infants classified as Bs, which is significantly fewer than the control group. There was also a difference in the pattern of anxious attachments between the two maltreatment groups. A significantly higher proportion of infants in the neglectful without physical abuse group were classified as Cs (57 percent); whereas 46 percent of the infants in the neglectful with physical abuse group were classified as As. The differences at eighteen months were not significant; however, some interesting changes occurred between twelve and eighteen months. The percentage of Bs remained low for both maltreatment groups. The big change was from 57 percent Cs at twelve months to 0 percent at eighteen months for the neglectful without physical abuse group. Half of the infants in this group (50 percent) became As at eighteen months.

At two years the differential effects of neglect alone and neglect with physical abuse were relatively small. The toddlers in the neglect without physical abuse group displayed more angry behavior, and those in the neglect with physical abuse group displayed more frustration behaviors. It is quite possible that they did not directly express their anger for fear of physical retaliation. Both groups displayed more negative and less positive affect than the controls. On the global ratings, both maltreatment groups obtained higher noncompliance, anger, and frustration with mother scores. The neglectful without physical abuse group obtained a significantly lower rating on the coping dimension.

Conclusion

Both the frequency of maltreatment in its various forms and the extent of its consequences were notable in this study. Our incidence figures are more likely underestimates than overestimates. First, as with other studies, we have had drop outs over the course of the investigation, although we have lost less than a third of the original sample. Since this is a prospective study, we have been able to test for early differences between those who later drop out and those who stay. There are predictable differences: In particular, more of the mothers who dropped out between twelve and eighteen months had anxiously attached infants. Had these mothers stayed in the study, our results would have been even more extreme. Second, only extreme and clearly documented cases were included in our maltreatment groups. Borderline cases were not. By going into the homes and getting to know the families, we discovered considerably more abuse and maltreatment than typically comes to the attention of local hospitals and other social agencies. In addition, while the incidence of maltreatment in our sample seems high, it is consistent with the extreme degree of stress and disorganization that characterize the lives of this poverty sample (Egeland, Breitenbucher, and Rosenberg, 1980). Finally, even though the different patterns of maltreatment were readily apparent, they did not exist in a "pure" form.

Documenting the consequences of maltreatment is important for social and legal purposes, but the most important aspect of our findings is not that maltreatment has negative consequences. That would seem a foregone conclusion, and the occurrence of maltreatment should in itself be sufficient to justify intervention. More important is establishing the particular consequences of physical abuse and broadening the conception of maltreatment. Even though the different forms of maltreatment had pervasive negative consequences, for most outcome variables, outcomes were related to particular patterns of maltreatment (see Cicchetti and Rizley, this volume).

The picture that emerged for the hostile group is very tentative since there were only four children in the hostile without physical abuse group. The quality of attachment for both the hostile groups did not differ greatly from the control group, even though, at eighteen months, there were significantly more securely attached infants in the control group. The outcome variables most affected by the hostile with and without physical abuse patterns were anger and frustration as observed at twenty-four months, while other expressions of affect (enthusiasm, positive and negative affect) seemed to be least affected.

The outcomes for the psychologically unavailable group seem severely malignant, pervasive, and pernicious. Having a mother who is chronically unavailable and unresponsive has devastating consequences on the child that touch every aspect of early functioning. Most strikingly, these children showed a declining pattern of functioning with every relevant assessment across the duration of the study. Their participation in the feeding and play situations declined, their BSID scores dropped dramatically, and the problems of attachment worsened. We are pessimistic about the futures of these children.

For the psychologically unavailable group, the outcomes were more homogeneous than was the case for the total physical abuse group. In addition to showing sharp declines in functioning, they were classified as having an anxious/avoidant pattern of attachment. At twenty-four months they were observed to be angry, frustrated, and noncompliant. Their threshold frustration was low, and they were emotionally unresponsive. This pattern of maltreatment seems to have a greater effect than any other form of maltreatment on emotional functioning.

It is difficult to explain why combining physical abuse with psychological unavailability resulted in seemingly less negative outcome than psychological unavailability alone. One possible explanation is that the contact that occurred in the form of physical abuse was better than no contact at all. It is possible that the mothers in the psychologically unavailable group are more emotionally detached and disinterested in their infants than the mothers in the psychologically unavailable with physical abuse group. The psychologically unavailable with physical abuse group may represent a form of ambivalence rather than total detachment and disinterest. It may also be true that the two psychologically unavailable groups differ on other dimensions of caretaking that were not considered in this investigation, or that later assessments show that outcomes for these groups differ not in degree but in kind. Some consequences of physical abuse may be more subtle and become apparent over time.

The effects of neglect were somewhat different than those of the other patterns of maltreatment, and the outcomes were different for neglect alone than for neglect combined with physical abuse. A large percentage of infants in the neglect alone group were classified as anxious/resistant at twelve months (Egeland and Sroufe, in press) while neglect with physical abuse infants tended to be classified anxious/avoidant. By eighteen months, infants in both neglect groups were likely to be classified as anxious/avoidant. At twenty-four months the neglect alone toddlers scored high on the anger rating, and the neglect and abuse groups were more likely to show frustration and whining. It is possible that the children in the neglect alone group express their frustration with mother's incompetence more directly in the form of anger; whereas the children in the neglect with physical abuse group display their frustration but do not express it directly in the form of anger for fear of mother's retaliation. Both neglect groups had a low coping score, which was not true for the other forms of maltreatment. The coping dimension pertains specifically to the degree of stress and frustration the child can tolerate. A high score on this scale indicates that the child stays organized in the face of challenge and frustration. A child receiving a low score becomes disorganized with minimum stress, and even with support the child is unable to engage the task.

The prevalence of anxious attachments at twelve and eighteen months and the anger, frustration, and opposition observed at twenty-four months for each pattern of maltreatment are noteworthy. These assessments are keyed to salient developmental issues, and the combination of outcome variables suggests serious problems with individuation and autonomy. Most two-year-olds assert their autonomy, but normally such assertiveness remains in balance with the ability to draw on parental support and with an enthusiasm in approaching the world. However, at a time when most children are engaging the environment on their own and falling back on caregivers when their own resources are exhausted, maltreated children are locked in an angry struggle with their caregivers or are unable to engage the environment effectively. These circumstances compromise the emergence of autonomy and the ability to engage the environment effectively. Even over two years there is a trend, particularly for the children in the psychologically unavailable group, to have increasing trouble with each developmental issue.

In many ways the pattern of declining functioning is the most important evidence we have uncovered. Although most children in the maltreatment groups were functioning at the normal developmental level at nine months, they appeared relatively retarded at twenty-four months. Moreover, those in the psychologically unavailable group were notably robust babies at three months, but even by six months their functioning declined markedly. This data clearly indicates that it was environmental factors rather than noxious child characteristics that underlay the negative developmental outcomes for these children. Assessments of child characteristics must begin very early in life. Had "temperament" assessments begun at six months, a very different conclusion would have been reached. By that time, and certainly by twenty-four months, the child may well be a contributing part of a very negative parent-child system. Yet, such negative contributions apparently were not part of the inherent constitution of the children. While we embrace a mutual influence-transactional model (Cicchetti and Rizley, this volume; Sameroff and Chandler, 1975), we nonetheless would argue that these findings strongly implicate quality of parenting in producing the negative outcomes observed. Some babies seem more resilient in the face of inadequate care, and some appear more vulnerable. On the whole, however, the maltreatment patterns defined had negative consequences for infants who, as a group, were not distinguished from the control infants in early assessments.

References

Ainsworth, M., Blehar, M., Waters, E., and Wall, S. *Patterns of Attachment.* Hillsdale, N.J.: Erlbaum, 1978.
Brunnquell, D., Crichton, L., and Egeland, B. "Maternal Personality and Attitude in Disturbances of Child-rearing." *American Journal of Orthopsychiatry,* in press.
Burgess, R., and Conger, R. "Family Interaction Patterns Related to Child Abuse and Neglect: Some Preliminary Findings." *Child Abuse and Neglect: The International Journal,* 1977, *1,* 269–277.
Cicchetti, D., Taraldson, B., and Egeland, B. "Perspectives in the Treatment and Understanding of Child Abuse." In A. Goldstein (Ed.), *Prescriptions for Child Mental Health and Education.* New York: Pergamon Press, 1978.
Egeland, B., Breitenbucher, M., and Rosenberg, D. "Prospective Study of the Significance of Life Stress in the Etiology of Child Abuse." *Journal of Consulting and Clinical Psychology,* 1980, *48* (2), 195–205.
Egeland, B., and Brunnquell, D. "An At-Risk Approach to the Study of Child Abuse: Some Preliminary Findings." *Journal of the American Academy of Child Psychiatry,* 1979, *18,* 219–235.
Egeland, B., Cicchetti, D., and Taraldson, B. "Child Abuse: A Family Affair." *Proceedings of the NP Masse Research Seminar on Child Abuse,* 28–52, Paris, France, 1976.
Egeland, B., and Deinard, A. "Child Care Rating Scale." Unpublished test, University of Minnesota, Minneapolis, 1975a.
Egeland, B., and Deinard, A. "A Prospective Study of the Antecedents of Child Abuse." Grant proposal, National Center on Child Abuse and Neglect. University of Minnesota, Minneapolis, 1975b.
Egeland, B., Deinard, A., and Sroufe, L. A. "Early Maladaptation: A Prospective-Transactional Study." Project proposal submitted to the Office of Maternal and Child Health, University of Minnesota, Minneapolis, Minnesota, 1977.
Egeland, B., and Sroufe, A. "Attachment and Early Maltreatment." *Child Development,* in press.
Elmer, E. *Fragile Families, Troubled Children.* Pittsburgh: University of Pittsburgh Press, 1977.
Galdston, R. "Observations on Children Who Have Been Physically Abused and Their Parents." *American Journal of Psychiatry,* 1965, *122,* 440–443.
Herrenkohl, R., and Herrenkohl, E. "Deficiency of Maternal Approval in the Abusive Family Environment." Unpublished paper, Lehigh University, Bethlehem, Pa., 1979.
Kempe, R., and Kempe, C. H. *Child Abuse.* London: Fontana/Open Books, 1978.

Martin, H. "The Child and His Development." In C. H. Kempe and R. E. Helfer (Eds.), *Helping the Battered Child and His Family.* Philadelphia: Lippincott, 1972.

Martin, H. P. (Ed.). *The Abused Child: Multidisciplinary Approach to Developmental Issues and Treatment.* Cambridge, Mass.: Ballinger, 1976.

Martin, H. P., and Beezeley, P. "Behavioral Observations of Abused Children." *Developmental Medicine and Child Neurology,* 1977, *19,* 373-387.

Martin, H. P., Beezeley, P., Conway, E. F., and Kempe, C. H. "The Development of Abused Children." *Advances in Pediatrics,* 1974, *21,* 25-73.

Matas, L., Arend, R. A., and Sroufe, L. A. "Continuity of Adaptation in the Second Year: The Relationship Between Quality of Attachment and Later Competence." *Child Development,* 1978, *49,* 547-556.

Morse, C. W., Sahler, O., and Friedman, S. "A Three-Year Follow-up Study of Abused and Neglected Children." *American Journal of Diseases of Children,* 1970, *120,* 439-446.

Ounsted, C., Oppenheimer, R., and Lindsay, J. "Aspects of Bonding Failure: The Psychopathological and Psychotherapeutic Treatment of Families of Battered Children." *Developmental Medicine and Child Neurology,* 1974, *16,* 447-456.

Parke, R. D., and Collmer, C. W. "Child Abuse: An Interdisciplinary Analysis." In E. M. Hetherington (Ed.), *Review of Child Development Research.* Vol. 5. Chicago: University of Chicago Press, 1975.

Sameroff, A., and Chandler, M. J. "Reproductive Risk and the Continuum of Caretaking Casualty." In F. D. Horowitz (Ed.), *Review of Child Development Research.* Chicago: University of Chicago Press, 1975.

Sandgrund, A., Gaines, R. W., and Green, A. H. "Child Abuse and Mental Retardation: A Problem of Cause and Effect." *American Journal of Mental Deficiency,* 1974, *79,* 327-330.

Terr, L. C. "A Family Study of Child Abuse." *American Journal of Psychiatry,* 1970, *127,* 125-131.

Vaughn, B., Taraldson, B., Crichton, L., and Egeland, B. "Relationships between Neonatal Behavioral Organization and Infant Behavior during the First Year of Life." *Infant Behavior and Development,* 1980, *3,* 47-66.

Waters, E. "The Reliability and Stability of Individual Differences in Infant-Mother Attachment." *Child Development,* 1978, *49,* 483-494.

Byron Egeland is the principal investigator of a longitudinal study of "high risk" children.

Alan Sroufe is the principle investigator on a project studying the preschool adjustment of children with varying developmental histories.

The risk of child maltreatment is increased by mitigation of parental solicitude that, in some circumstances, can be predicted from evolutionary theory.

Child Maltreatment from a Sociobiological Perspective

Martin Daly
Margo I. Wilson

> According to an inclusive-fitness model, selection should refine parental altruism as if in response to three hypothetical cost-benefit questions: (1) What is the genetic relationship of the putative offspring to its parents? (Is the juvenile really my own offspring?) (2) What is the need of the offspring? (More properly, what is its ability to translate parental assistance into reproduction?) (3) What alternative uses might a parent make of the resources it can invest in the offspring? (Alexander, 1979, p. 109)

In the United States in 1976, children living with a natural parent and a stepparent were several times as likely to be victims of physical abuse as were children living with both natural parents (Wilson, Daly, and Weghorst, 1980). This phenomenon of elevated risk in stephouseholds appears to be widespread. In a Swedish government report cited by Vesterdal (1978), for exam-

We thank Judy Thompson and the London Family Consultant Service for use of the data in Figure 1, and the Harry Frank Guggenheim Foundation for research support.

ple, stepfathers were perpetrators in some 19 percent of those physical abuse cases for which the culprits were identified. Out of 255 hospitalized victims of severe physical abuse in New Zealand, 105 (41 percent) lived with one or more substitute parents (Fergusson, Fleming, and O'Neill, 1972). And more than 20 percent of a sample of 1194 battered English children lived with a stepfather (Creighton and Owtram, 1977).

Less violent forms of child maltreatment ("neglect") are also associated with stepparenting, though to a lesser extent than is physical abuse (Wilson, Daly, and Weghorst, 1980); child neglect in America (which the American Humane Association defines broadly to include abandonment, lack of supervision, emotional, medical and educational neglect, among others) is instead most strongly associated with the absence of one parent. Data from a Canadian study (Figure 1) illustrate the same points.

The association between substitute parenting and risk of maltreatment will come as no surprise to those familiar with evolutionary biology. The complex and costly repertoire of parental care has evolved in the service of raising own offspring. It is to be expected that the motivational underpinnings of adequate parenting will be sensitive to the distinction between own and alien young, since those who expend parental resources on unrelated young will raise fewer of their own and will lose out in the reproductive competition that is natural selection. Stepparents cannot be expected to abandon themselves to their role, and indeed human stepparents cannot easily do so: in a Cleveland study, for example, Duberman (1975) found that only 53 percent of stepfathers and 25 percent of stepmothers professed "parental feelings" toward their wards.

Nonhuman animals also manifest discriminative parental solicitude (Daly and Wilson, 1980a). In one exemplary study, royal terns were found to recognize and incubate their own eggs which an experimenter had moved to a neighbor's nest, while neglecting the alien eggs artificially placed in their own nests (Buckley and Buckley, 1972). These birds nest in dense colonies and eggs are sometimes displaced in the absence of experimental intervention. Other studies have shown that some densely nesting sea birds recognize their eggs and chicks while related species with dispersed nest sites do not (Birkhead, 1978; but see Pierotti, 1980). In general, individual recognition of one's own young seems to be well developed where it counts, that is to say in those species and in those stages of development where mixups and misdirected parental care are genuine risks in the natural circumstance. Adaptive control mechanisms of parental behavior thus appear to have evolved to ensure that parents invest in their own offspring rather than the offspring of their reproductive competitors.

We believe that the inclination to invest preferentially in own young is the basis for the association between stepparenting and maltreatment risk. We are not going to argue that child maltreatment is adaptive. We will, however,

Figure 1. Categorization of Family Crises Leading to Police Calls, According to Household Composition and Case Workers' Reports of Evidence of Child Maltreatment

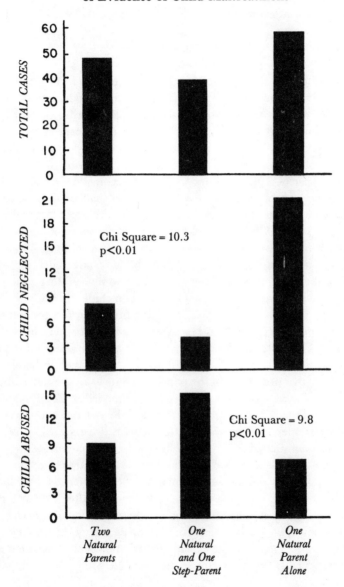

Chi Square = 10.3
p<0.01

Chi Square = 9.8
p<0.01

Note: The data represent 144 cases investigated by the Family Consultant Service of London, Ontario, Canada; these were all the cases for which household composition was recorded, during a six-month period in 1978, out of 177 involving focal individuals under eighteen years of age. Physical abuse risk is elevated in stepparent households, while neglect risk is elevated in single parent households (in comparison to "expected" values proportionate to total case frequencies).

suggest that the risk of maltreatment is exacerbated by a variety of circumstances in which some mitigation of parental solicitude—some reluctance to commit parental resources—was adaptive in the selective milieu of hominid evolution. This argument rests upon the theoretical perspective outlined below.

The Sociobiological View of Organisms

Biologists are convinced that life forms are the products of evolution by natural selection, hence of a history of differential reproductive success. An implication of this basic tenet is that evolved adaptive attributes must contribute, however indirectly, to their carriers' reproductive prospects (at least insofar as the selective milieu within which the attributes evolved persists). The adaptive functions of a characteristic are likely to be intelligible only within a broader context of a species-typical "strategy." Bipedal locomotion in hominids, for example, is presumably adaptively related to open habitat, a gathering and hunting way of life, and the developing use of the hands and material culture.

Organisms may be viewed as strategies, designed by natural selection to behave as if in response to a series of cost-benefit decisions. They choose among alternative courses of action on the basis of any reliable predictive information that they are capable of garnering and interpreting. The predictive information that should be acted upon might include correlations between daylight and predation risk, season and mating prospects, hunger and acceptable risk of poisoning, perceived resemblance and probability of paternity, and so forth. The costs and benefits that matter are ultimately reproductive: One expends a portion of one's accrued energy or survival probability, and hence reproductive prospects, in the pursuit of returns in the same currency, namely successful reproduction. This economic model of the ultimate rationale for behavioral strategies has been developed by many authors (see, for example, Alexander, 1979; MacFarland, 1977; Trivers, 1972; Williams, 1966) and has dominated recent research in animal behavior.

Organisms are also said to have "life history strategies," which are adaptive schedules for the expenditure of reproductive effort over the lifetime. Maturity may be early or delayed. Parents may die after exhausting their resources in a single breeding episode or may breed repeatedly. Each species, including our own, has a characteristic life history strategy. Much sociobiological theory is concerned with the explanation of interspecific variation in life-historical parameters (see for example, Stearns, 1976).

Human Life History Strategy

The *Homo sapiens* reproductive strategy is one of prolonged, intensive nurture of a few widely spaced children. If our species has indeed evolved a characteristic life history, with which psychological processes such as parental attachment and social development have become coadapted during evolution, then we should like to know if any present-day human populations are good models of ancestral *Homo sapiens*. The likeliest candidates are peoples still occupying the ecological niche characteristic of our long prehistory, namely hunting and gathering. The best studied such people, and one whose world is perhaps as close as any to the ancestral hominids', is the Kalahari !Kung San.

The San exhibit a loose territorial and band structure (Lee and DeVore, 1976). Predominantly monogamous nuclear families are the permanent units out of which the typical village aggregation of about thirty and forty kinfolk assemble. Marriage and child bearing are virtually universal among women. In the !Kung San population studied by Howell (1979) menarche occurs at a mean age of 16.6 years and the first child is most commonly born at a maternal age of nineteen years. San births are few and widely spaced: Harpending (1976) reports 4.65 live births by menopause. The San evidently lack effective contraception or abortion practices. Howell (1976) reports six cases of infanticide out of 500 live births; precipitating circumstances include birth abnormalities, failure of lactational birth spacing, and the birth of twins. (The rationality of prompt infanticide in such circumstances is a question to which we shall return.) About 20 percent of newborns do not survive the first year, with gastrointestinal and respiratory diseases and malaria the leading causes of mortality.

Those children who are reared receive no paucity of nurturant attention (Konner, 1977). Nursing commonly continues until age four and exceptionally until age six (Howell, 1976). Infants are carried in a sling, and suckle on a demand schedule with a mean of four bouts per hour and two minutes per bout during daylight hours; this nursing schedule did not change greatly through 139 weeks postpartum (Konner and Worthman, 1980). A three-month old baby spends perhaps 80 percent of the day and all the night in direct physical contact with its mother; at a year, such contact still occupies about half the day (Konner, 1976). The nursing schedule evidently suppresses maternal ovarian function and delays the next conception (Konner and Worthman, 1980). When pregnancy recurs, after perhaps three or four years, the nursing infant is weaned, often with considerable protest, and the focus of its social experience rather abruptly switches from mother to other children, in whose company it spends virtually all its waking hours (Draper, 1976; Konner, 1976). A group of adults, especially women, supervises the multiaged play group of children informally but continuously (Draper, 1976). According to Howell (1979), "The !Kung show great restraint in physical violence against children. All observers agree that !Kung parents are extremely nonpunitive with their children, and even tolerant when little children occasionally slap or insult their parents" (p. 62). One hypothesis suggested by these observations is that physical abuse of children is extremely rare in "natural" social milieus.

Howell (1979) has cautioned against considering the San "typical" hunter-gatherers and hence human prototypes. However, limited evidence suggests that the child-care practices of other hunter-gatherers are similar. Lozoff and Brittenham (1979) contrasted ten hunter-gatherer societies, 176 other nonindustrial societies, and the United States. Several features that are almost universal among hunger-gatherers are almost unheard of in America (while preindustrial agricultural societies tend to be intermediate); these include extensive and prolonged mother-infant contact (including sleeping together), demand nursing continued beyond two years of age, an immediate nurturant reponse to crying, and a weaning transition to membership in a play group of children. Konner (1977) has discussed possible developmental consequences of such variations in childhood experience.

Abortion and Infanticide Reviewed Cross-Culturally

With the invention of agriculture only a few thousand years ago came radical modifications of women's reproductive activity, including the possibility of early weaning and shortened birth intervals, largely as a result of changes in maternal nutrition and available food supplements for infants. Where a successful gatherer might raise six surviving children, agricultural woman might raise a dozen. But children too numerous or in too rapid succession will have remained a burden that was sometimes intolerable. Both deliberate infanticide (see below) and more ambivalently motivated child abuse and neglect (Daly and Wilson, 1980b) occur when a woman's resources — material, temporal and human — are overextended.

The ethnographic literature is simply inadequate to document the incidence of child abuse in different societies. Descriptions of childrearing practices are vague and often ethnocentrically evaluative. Any cross-cultural tabulation encounters definitional diffculties as well. Is ritual mutilation "abuse," for example? And should one decide on the basis of whether it is inflicted on all or only select children, at just one occasion or more chronically? We will not attempt to review child maltreatment cross-culturally (but see Barry and Paxson, 1971; Langer, 1974; Thomas, 1972). A more manageable task is a review of the prevalence of infanticide and abortion in human societies and of the circumstances in which they occur. For this purpose, we have used the HRAF (Human Relations Area Files) Probability Sample Files. This is a sample of sixty human societies which has been devised by cultural anthropologists to represent, according to several criteria, an unbiased sample of the world's cultures (Lagacé, 1974). Table 1 presents a summary of HRAF information on infanticide and abortion in these sixty societies.

In several of the cases, the act of infanticide was carried out by the mother, but in several others a midwife or other party committed the deed.

Table 1. Abortion and Infanticide in the Sixty Societies of the
"Probability Sample Files," According to Information in the
Human Relations Area Files

	No. of Societies Where Practice Is Observed	Birth Abnormality	Burdensome (Twins, Too Many Children, Too Soon After Previous Child)	Unwed Mother	Adultery
Infanticide	39	22	24	14	15
Abortion	34	0	11	24	6
Infanticide or Abortion	48	22	30	26	19

The four most prevalent classes of precipitating circumstances are indicated; table entries represent the number of societies in which the labelled circumstance is described as grounds for infanticide or abortion.

Not infrequently, mothers were described as balking at actually killing their infants, but achieved the same end quickly by neglect.

The four precipitating circumstances in Table 1 can each be considered intelligible "reproductive strategic" grounds for termination of a parental episode. We will return to the subjects of defective children and adulterous conceptions later, but wish first to draw attention to the maternal resource situation. The most frequent grounds for infanticide and abortion ("unwed" and "burdensome") are matters of maternal incapacity to cope. In fourteen of our sixty societies, the ethnographer notes that one or both of twins are routinely killed; Granzberg (1973) has shown that "twin infanticide is typically found in societies where mothers have a heavy workload and where they have a minimal amount of help" (p. 411), and is rare elsewhere. In ten of our sixty societies, infanticide was said to be provoked by children too numerous or in too rapid succession, and abortion for the same reason was noted in seven. Infanticide upon the death of the mother was recorded in seven cases.

In societies, such as our own, in which disposal of burdensome infants is not an option, poverty and overtaxing of maternal resources exacerbate risk of both physical abuse and neglect, but especially the latter (Garbarino, 1976; Pelton, 1978; Wilson, Daly, and Weghorst, 1980).

Commonality and Conflict of Interest

Sociobiological theory affords a general explanation for variation from parental solicitousness to neglect. The most important stimulus to the recent development of sociobiological theory was W. D. Hamilton's (1964) formulation of the concept of "inclusive fitness." Hamilton perceived that offspring, the usual "currency" in which fitness (reproductive success) had been measured, are only a subset of the relatives in whose welfare a focal individual might invest. In terms of gene replication, a contribution to a full sibling has exactly the same natural selective consequences as a like contribution to an offspring; contributions to more distant relatives are selectively devalued according to precise coefficients of relatedness which represent commonality of genotype. The "inclusive fitness" consequences of an individual's behavior therefore include not only personal reproductive success, but also any influences upon the reproductive success of relatives, weighted according to the degrees of relatedness. Hamilton's analysis broadened the sociobiological conception of organisms from "reproductive strategies" to *nepotistic* strategists" (see Alexander, 1979).

In terms of natural selection, an organism's "self-interest" reduces to the promotion of inclusive fitness. This is so even though the organism may be motivated by more immediate goals, since the motivational mechanisms have evolved to promote inclusive fitness. *Commonality* of interest then boils down to this question: to what extent does that which promotes my inclusive fitness also promote yours? *Conflict* of interest, conversely, is the extent to which either of us promotes his own inclusive fitness at the other's expense.

By these definitions, only genetically identical individuals have perfect commonality — and no conflict — of interest. (It follows that we should find no child abuse in clones and asexually reproducing species.) In sexual reproducers such as ourselves, relatives are not genetically identical (with the exception of monozygotic twins whose existence has probably been without selective significance in human evolution) and they therefore necessarily have both commonality and conflict of interest. This is the fundamental point of the parent-offspring conflict theory advanced by Robert Trivers (1974). Parental behavior and motives should have evolved to distribute parental investment (Trivers, 1972) among offspring, and other relatives, in a manner optimal for the inclusive fitness of the parent. An offspring, however, may be expected to covet a larger share of parental benevolence than the parent willingly offers. According to this theory, weaning conflict and indeed parent-offspring conflict throughout the relationship is an inevitable consequence of genetic nonidentity, though both parties will have evolved compromise tactics to minimize the costs.

A deduction from parent-offspring conflict theory is that parents in sexually reproducing species should not exhibit automatic nurturant responses to the entreaties of their offspring. Instead, they should attempt to assess the offspring's true need, and should allocate their parental investment in such a way as to maximize their own inclusive fitness. If this strategy demands the occasional neglect of dependent infants to save either more advanced dependent offspring or the parent's own reproductive future, then the capacity for such neglect may be expected to have evolved. In many bird species, for example, nestlings compete for the food that parents bring, with the result that size disparities increase and runts starve rather quickly when resources are poor; it is only when hunting is good enough for the largest to become sated that the parents feed the runts. In such species, parents may withhold feeding until the resolution of a begging competition among the nestlings.

Offspring Quality and Parental Inclination

What we are arguing is that the motivational mechanisms controlling parental behavior have evolved in such a way that parents will act as if they value a particular offspring in direct proportion to that offspring's expected contribution to parental inclusive fitness. That expected contribution equals the product of the offspring's "reproductive value" times its "coefficient of relatedness" to the parent. The "reproductive value" is a measure of expected future reproduction, and depends upon viability and prospects for fecundity, hence upon both environmental circumstances and the intrinsic quality of the organism. It also depends upon the stage of development that has been attained, increasing as the youngster approaches maturity merely by virtue of the increasing probability that older surviving offspring will survive to breed. The "coefficient of relatedness" is usually 0.5 but the probability may be reduced in the case of doubt of paternity, in the same case of substitute parenting by a more distant relative such as grandparent or mother's brother, and so on. Parents should have evolved to "estimate" (consciousness not implied) these quantities according to whatever information they can gather, and to value their offspring accordingly.

Clear signs of poor offspring quality may be expected to counteract the development of parental solicitude. Birds abandon cracked eggs and parturient rodents devour moribund neonates. However, there are fewer clear cases of parental abandonment of inferior offspring in the animal behavior literature, particularly in the case of mammals, than one might expect, and there are even descriptions of primate mothers carrying and grooming dead infants for several days (Lindburg, 1971; van Lawick-Goodall, 1971).

Part of the explanation for the paucity of examples of termination of investment in relatively advanced young surely lies in the commitment of parental resources required by young at different stages of development. The nearer the dependent offspring is to independence—and a major portion of requisite parental investment may already have been expended by birth—the less further parental investment is required to reach successful weaning. Both this fact and the maturing young's increasing reproductive value should tend to elevate the parental threshold for abandonment. This prediction has been supported by studies measuring risks endured by nesting birds: Parents accept increasing risks of predation in defending helpless offspring the closer they are to independent maturity (Andersson, Wiklund, and Rundgren, 1980; Barash, 1975; Greig-Smith, 1980). The same principle should hold with respect to threshold levels of offspring impairment for parental abandonment, though a perfectly "rational" reproductive strategist would abandon a *hopelessly* defective offspring at whatever stage. It may also be the case that particular defects are either difficult to discern or have occurred so rarely in the evolutionary history of the species in question that parents have not evolved the capacity to discriminate against them.

Another reason for adaptive variation in parental inclination to invest in particular offspring could be life-span developmental changes in the parent's own reproductive prospects (see for example, Pianka and Parker, 1975). An aging parent has a declining residual reproductive value, which means simply a declining expectation of future reproduction. An older parent therefore risks less inclusive fitness than a younger parent when the two perform identical acts that incur the same personal mortality risks and energetic costs. It follows that older parents might have different thresholds of tolerable risk and of offspring quality controlling their parental behavior. One prediction from such a view is that pregnant nulliparous women, informed of a complication with specified risks, will opt for abortion decreasingly as a function of age (Barash 1976a; see also Lenington, 1979). Similarly, insofar as cases of child abuse and neglect derive from parents resenting their obligations to particular children, we might expect that the probability of maltreatment of children with particular defects will decline with maternal age, and will increase when other children (alternative recipients of parental investment) are present. These life historical predictions are not rigorously derived, and it might be plausible to argue, conversely, that a reproductive strategist nearing menopause will be particularly impatient to terminate a poor-risk investment and get on with the next one. These are empirically researchable alternatives.

For twenty-two of the sixty human societies in the "Probability Sample Files," the ethnographic reports in the HRAF mention infanticide in the event of birth abnormalities (Table 1; see also Dickemann, 1975). Expressed rationales for this practice range from doubts about the child's viability to fears of monsters and disastrous magical consequences. Where society obliges parents to rear seriously defective infants, risks of neglect and abuse are high. Daly and Wilson (1980b) review evidence that children with congenital handicaps are disproportionately victimized and that institutionalized defective children have a high probability of being effectively abandoned by their families.

It remains an open question to what extent such parental mistreatment is directly evoked by characteristics of the child. Whether the baby is normal is a first concern of parturient women, and there is certainly evidence of parental shock and rejection upon being presented with an obviously defective child

(Drotar, Baskiewicz, Irvin, Kennell, and Klaus, 1975; Fletcher, 1974). When such children are raised at home, the probability of marriage break-up is elevated (for example, Martin, 1975; Tew, Payne, and Laurence, 1974). However, birth defects also tend to be associated with postnatal mother-infant separation, and there are grounds for concluding that such separation is itself a cause of child abuse (see "the maternal bonding failure hypothesis" below).

Sex-biased Parental Investment

A classic problem in evolutionary biology is the adaptive significance of the sex ratio. Why are females and males about equally numerous? Fisher (1958) provided the generally accepted solution to this question: Since each individual has a male and female parent, the two sexes contribute equally to future generations and hence are equally valuable to the parents as inclusive fitness vehicles. If the sex ratio becomes imbalanced, then the average reproductive success of individuals of the rare sex surpasses that of the common sex, so that production of the rare sex is selectively favored, pushing the sex ratio back toward equality.

There are some instructive exceptions. When sibling males will simply compete for the same fertilizations ("local mate competition"), as in the case of certain parasitic insects where males inseminate their sisters, then the best parental strategy for maximizing grandchild production will be to produce mostly females and few or even a single son, and that is what occurs (Hamilton, 1967). This example also points up the fact that females are the limiting sex in terms of reproductive capacity; number of males is seldom as important a determinant of population productivity.

A further qualification to the expectation of equal number of daughters and sons was noted by Fisher (1958). This is the case where one or the other sex is more "expensive" for the parents to produce. If two sons, for example, can be produced for the same expenditure of effort as one daughter, then the equilibrium sex ratio will be two males to one female, with an average son only half as "valuable" (in terms of expected grandchild units) as an average daughter but also only half as costly. This consideration is relevant in species in which female and male producing eggs contain different initial amounts of energy, or in which male and female nestlings are fed different amounts (see, for example, Howe, 1977).

An important extension of Fisher's theory was advanced by Trivers and Willard (1973) who pointed out that whereas the equilibrium sex ratio may be unity for the population, individual parents might be expected to adjust their own offspring sex ratios according to circumstance. Males generally exhibit greater variance in fitness than females (Bateman, 1948; Trivers, 1972): most surviving female offspring become breeders, while disadvantaged male offspring remain celibate, and the better-situated males fertilize many females. It follows that an effective parental strategy may entail production of males when the parent is in good condition and is best able to provide sons with a good start, and production of females at other times. Moreover, where both sons and daughters are present, the sex difference in fitness variance will often mean that surplus parental resources yield better returns when invested in sons rather than daughters, a consideration which may be relevant to male-preferential inheritance (Hartung, 1976).

Dickemann (1979), following a suggestion by Alexander (1974), has applied Trivers and Willard's theory to the distribution of female-selective infanticide in stratified human societies. The practice proves to be status graded, with the highest classes removing substantial proportions of daughters, while investing in sons who have prospects for polygamous unions and high reproductive success. Women (and their families) strive to achieve upwardly mobile marriages and liaisons, while men in the lowest echelons are likely to remain consigned to celibacy. Dickemann's analysis therefore also suggests the possibility of male-selective infanticide and destructive neglect in hard times and in the lowest classes, a phenomenon not yet documented. Lenington (1979) has predicted on the same grounds that the proportion of female victims of abuse will increase with increasing socioeconomic status; this prediction has yet to be tested.

In America, boys and girls are indeed differentially abused (Wilson, Daly and Weghorst, in press) but the pattern of sex differences is complex. Among the youngest infants, girls are more often victimized, but by age two this difference is reversed; in adolescence, girls are again the principal victims, partly but not entirely because of sexual abuse. These vicissitudes warrant examination in relation to economic variables.

In the case of adolescent girls, relatively high abuse risk may be a result of parental double standards concerning both acceptable behavior and the use of punishment. Teenage girls, in comparison to boys, are given less freedom with respect to activities and choice of friends, perhaps because of parental concern with daughters' chastity, reputation, and marriageability (Dickemann, 1980; Wilson, Daly, and Weghorst, in press).

Paternity Concern

Double standards concerning sexual morality derive from a basic biological asymmetry: whereas females in natural circumstances are seldom susceptible to mistakes in identifying their offspring, males can be cuckolded and hence deceived about paternity. In any species in which males invest significantly in the welfare of young, they may be expected to have evolved a variety of tactics for the accurate assessment and defense of paternity. In studies of biparental birds, for example, males have been shown: (1) to expend considerable time and effort in guarding their mates when they are fertilizable and in pursuing adulterous opportunity at other times (Beecher and Beecher, 1979; Cheng, Burns, and McKinney, 1980); (2) to reject as mates those females previously courted and therefore possibly inseminated by other males (Erickson and Zenone, 1976); (3) to attack their mates as well as the male intruders upon discovering circumstantial evidence of possible adultery (Barash, 1976b; Gowaty, 1979; Zenone, 1980); and (4) to pair with widowed females while offering no assistance to the offspring of their predecessors (Power, 1975).

Beyond merely refraining from investing in another's young, it may behoove a male to dispose of them. Male lions who take over a pride displace the former breeding males, retain the mature females, and kill the cubs (Bertram, 1975); such infanticide promotes the fitness of its perpetrators by terminating lactation and thus hastening a return to estrus and fecundability in the mothers. Much the same story has been documented for langur monkeys in India, and there is growing evidence that such infanticidal behavior is widespread among primates (Hrdy, 1979).

Human males are profoundly concerned with paternity and especially the paternity of those children on whom they are called upon to invest. This is surely the basis for the cross-culturally prevalent double standard in penalties for adultery (Daly and Wilson, 1979) and for the value attached to female virginity. As Dickemann (1979) has shown, families in several stratified societies compete to marry their daughters upward by demonstrations of their capacity to raise girls who "value and manifest ideals of feminine modesty, purity, and shame" (p. 173). The rejection of a "sullied" bride can have disastrous consequences for the future marital ambitions of her kin, and male "honor" is linked to the chastity of female relatives (see for example, Safilios-Rothschild, 1969). The means of enforcing female purity that are routinely practiced in many societies would constitute child abuse in our own; these range from confinement to clitoridectomy and crippling foot binding (Dickemann, 1979). We have already suggested that abuse of adolescent girls in our own society may derive in part from similar parental motives.

Where men do not insist on virginal wives, they can still avoid investing in another man's children. In societies in which paternity confidence is not attainable, men redirect "parental" investment into known kin, namely their sister's children rather than their wives' children (Kurland, 1979). More commonly, men still try to monopolize their wives' reproductive effort. When a Tikopia man acquired a wife with an infant from a previous marriage, he would order the infant killed and he justified his action by demanding "Whose is this child for whom I must fetch food from the woods?" (Firth, 1936, p. 529). The same practice with a similarly straightforward rationale has been described for Yanomamö (Chagnon, 1968). Nor need we go to the ethnographic litera-

106

ture for examples. We recently observed a sample of videotaped human births in a study of abuse risk in relation to behavior around parturition. In one case, the mother was extremely anxious about the racial appearance of the baby. It turned out that she had conceived at about the time of a change of mates and had a proposal of marriage from her current man that was explicitly contingent upon paternity. It would be interesting to investigate whether the victim, in those families in which one child is singled out for abuse, is the child least resembling the father.

The exacerbation of child abuse risk in stephouseholds (Wilson, Daly, and Weghorst, 1980) may be hypothesized to derive largely from resentment of the obligation to invest parentally in others' children. An analysis of maltreatment type in relation to household composition (Daly and Wilson, 1980b) suggests that such resentment may be a special element in the causation of abuse: Given that children were mistreated seriously enough for the case to be reported to the American Humane Association, the probability that they were physically injured—hence that there was a violent rather than just neglectful component—was less than one in three in households containing only adults related to the victim and greater than one in two where an unrelated adult (stepparent, foster parent, adoptive parent—usually a male) was present.

If attacks from unrelated males are a frequent threat to infants, then protection against such attack should become an important criterion of female mate selection. There is then selective pressure for females to establish prolonged associations with powerful males and to provide those males with confidence of paternity. Protection from attack may then be the major form of paternal investment in offspring. Such a selective history has been suggested as a formative influence in several primate social systems (reviewed by Hrdy, 1979) and in human society (Alexander, 1979).

In Table 1 we noted that adultery is considered grounds for infanticide or abortion in at least nineteen of sixty societies. In three of these societies, infants whose appearance indicated a nontribal sire were killed. Elsewhere, adulterous conception was considered grounds for murder or expulsion of the woman and child together, and for disinheritance, abuse and enslavement of the child. In several of the sixty societies, a ritual of parental acknowledgement of the child was described. Children who were not so acknowledged might be allowed to live, but were often lifelong pariahs lacking rights to property and marriage.

The Maternal-Bonding Failure Hypothesis

Given the opportunity, human mothers and infants commonly interact immediately after birth in a rather stereotyped way including intense eye contact (Klaus, Trause, and Kennell, 1975; Klaus and Kennell, 1976). After intensive contact with their infants over the first few days, new mothers commonly report developing a feeling that the child is special and wonderful, whereas mothers separated from their infants frequently report feeling emotionally detached from the child (Kennell, Trause, and Klaus, 1975). It has thus been suggested that the immediate postnatal period is especially important in the development of an individualized mother-infant bond, and that modern birth practices may disrupt this process (see for example, Sugarman, 1977).

In a series of experimental hospital studies, reviewed by Klaus and Kennell (1976), Lozoff, Brittenham, Trause, Kennell, and Klaus (1977), and Richards (1978), mothers have been randomly assigned to limited contact "hospital routine" versus "rooming-in" conditions in the maternity hospital. The greater neonatal contact afforded by the rooming-in condition has then been shown to influence subsequent behavior and child development according to a variety of measures.

The above facts suggest the hypothesis that neonatal separation may contribute to child abuse risk. Certainly separation and risk are associated. Lynch (1975), for example, found that 40 percent of a sample of severely abused children had been separated from their mothers during their first forty-eight hours compared to just 6 percent of their nonabused siblings. Premature children and others with various defects are high-risk groups that also experience neonatal separation (reviewed by Daly and Wilson, 1980b), but such evidence is ambiguous due to its correlational nature. One experimental hospital study, however, provides some dramatic, direct evidence. Low-income primiparous women were assigned to "hospital routine" versus "rooming-in" conditions for the first two days postpartum (O'Connor, Vietze, Hopkins, and Altemeier, 1977; O'Connor, Vietze, Sherrod, Sandler, and Altemeier, 1979). The manipulation entailed an extra six hours mother-infant contact per day for the latter group. In follow-up studies in the second year, nine of the 143 "hospital routine" children were categorized as victims of abuse, neglect, abandonment, or nonorganic failure to thrive, compared to none of 134 "rooming-in" children. If these consequences of rooming-in experience prove to be reliable, then prevention of child maltreatment must be a major justification for the provision of more "natural" postnatal contact experience for mothers and infants.

Adaptation and Human Behavior

Infanticide was documented in thirty-nine of the sixty societies that we reviewed from the HRAF. We found over one hundred expressed rationales for infanticide (including those repeated in different societies) and only seven of those did not make clear reproductive strategic sense. While that in itself constitutes strong support for the sociobiological perspective, even those seven are probably not cases in which people are acting against their inclusive fitness. In one case (Baganda), chiefs killed their first child if it was a son, apparently to avoid a premature bid to supplant the father. In three more cases, magical rationales were offered (to assuage the gods, and so on), but nothing was said about the mode of selection of victims, whom we would hypothesize to have been selected on the same reproductive strategic grounds as operate elsewhere. This leaves three truly surprising allegations: that Lau men kill their sister's sons to escape the obligation to provide them brides; that Mataco men kill their own grandsons if displeased with their sons-in-law; and that Yanomamö men may kill their own children in order to end their wives' lactational taboo period and resume sexual relations. Each of these may represent a real instance of cultural practice in conflict with individual reproductive self-interest, but we doubt it. We predict instead that further research would reveal each of these cases to be deceptively described—that the practices are not prevalent, that the sisters are classificatory rather than biological kin, that the real precipitating circumstances are concealed.

Sociobiologists have been accused of believing, like Dr. Pangloss in Voltaire's *Candide,* that all is for the best in this best of all possible worlds. Whatever behavior we encounter, we can invent an adaptive story to explain it, and if we discover the converse in the next species or society, why, that's adaptive too. The criticism is overstated, but it contains an element of truth. The ground rules for identifying evolutionary adaptation, especially in behavior, remain elusive. A major problem is that the foundation of behavioral science is weak: We often lack satisfactory description, categorization, and identification of appropriate units at appropriate levels of abstraction. All *individual* acts are unique events, some of which are fitness-enhancing while others are not. The claim of adaptation is a claim about the average fitness consequences of a class of acts. When we argue, for example, that infanticide by male langurs is adaptive, we are making a claim about a class of acts. How are we to decide if this classification is at an appropriate level, that is to say a level at which heritable variation and relevant natural selection have occurred? Perhaps it is not in behavioristically defined acts but in emotional responses to classes of circumstances that we should seek adaptation. Is it more accurate and useful, for example, to hypothesize that resentment of filial solicitations from unrelated young has evolved? Some critics (for example, Lewontin, 1979) have argued that because behavior is not physical structure it cannot be said to evolve at all, but this is surely too pessimistic a position. Nevertheless we need more sophisticated attention to the question of what exactly is alleged to have evolved.

A related problem is that of "natural environments" (Symons, 1979). The claim of adaptation is in fact a claim about the average fitness consequences of a class of acts in historical environments where selection occurred.

Even more difficult than adequate description of behavior is adequate description of relevant environmental circumstances. Do modern people live in circumstances that are similar enough to ancestral ones that their behavior tends to be adaptive? In some ways they must, for they are surviving and reproducing, but technology can be argued to have subverted fitness-promoting inclinations, perhaps most clearly in the example of birth control. At what level of abstraction can modern sociocultural circumstances be described as retaining essential features of "natural" ones?

A final word about the relationship between conscious motives and reproductive strategies. It has become a sociobiological cliche to disclaim the implication of conscious intent in the use of the strategy metaphor. That disclaimer is appropriate, but it is not enough. We and other authors have quoted people's expressed rationales for their behavior where they seemed to support the equation of self-interest with inclusive fitness. But in other cases people's words are distinctly "irrational" from the viewpoint of reproductive strategies, and we are still a long way from having a powerful theory that predicts where the two will and will not jibe. We look forward to progress toward an evolutionary psychology (see Crook, 1980).

References

Alexander, R. D. "The Evolution of Social Behavior." *Annual Review of Ecology and Systematics*, 1974, *5*, 325-383.

Alexander, R. D. *Darwinism and Human Affairs*. Seattle: University of Washington Press, 1979.

Andersson, M., Wiklund, C. G., and Rundgren, H. "Parental Defence of Offspring: A Model and an Example." *Animal Behaviour*, 1980, *28*, 536-542.

Barash, D. P. "Evolutionary Aspects of Parental Behavior: The Distraction Display of the Alpine Accentor, *Prunella Collaris*." *Wilson Bulletin*, 1975, *87*, 367-373.

Barash, D. P. "Some Evolutionary Aspects of Parental Behavior in Animals and Man." *American Journal of Psychology*, 1976a, *89*, 195-217.

Barash, D. P. "Male Response to Apparent Female Adultery in the Mountain Bluebird *(Siala Currocoides)*: An Evolutionary Interpretation." *American Naturalist*, 1976b, *110*, 1097-1101.

Barry, H., and Paxson, L. M., "Infancy and Early Childhood: Cross-Cultural Codes 2." *Ethnology*, 1971, *10*, 466-508.

Bateman, A. J. "Intra-sexual Selection in *Drosophila*." *Heredity*, 1948, *2*, 349-368.

Beecher, M. D., and Beecher, I. M. "Sociobiology of Bank Swallows: Reproductive Strategy of the Male." *Science*, 1979, *205*, 1282-1285.

Bertram, B. C. R. "Social Factors Influencing Reproduction in Wild Lions." *Journal of Zoology*, 1975, *177*, 463-482.

Birkhead, T. R. "Behavioral *Uria Aalge*." *Animal Behaviour*, 1978, *26*, 321-331.

Buckley, P. A., and Buckley, F. G. "Individual Egg and Chick Recognition by Adult Royal Terns *(Sterna Maxima Maxima)*." *Animal Behaviour*, 1972, *20*, 457-462.

Chagnon, N. A. *Yanomamö: the Fierce People*. New York: Holt, Rinehart and Winston, 1968.

Cheng, K. M., Burns, J. T., and McKinney, F. "Forced Copulation in Captive Mallards." Paper presented at Animal Behavior Society, Fort Collins, Colorado, June 9-13, 1980.

Creighton, S. J., and Owtram, P. J. *Child Victims of Physical Abuse. A Report on the Findings of NSPCC Special Units' Registers.* London: National Society for the Prevention of Cruelty to Children, 1977.

Crook, J. H. *The Evolution of Human Consciousness.* Oxford: Clarendon Press, 1980.

Daly, M., and Wilson, M. "Sex and Strategy." *New Scientist,* 1979, *81* (1136), 15-17.

Daly, M., and Wilson, M. "Discriminative Parental Solicitude: A Biological Perspective." *Journal of Marriage and the Family,* 1980a, *42,* 277-288.

Daly, M., and Wilson, M. "Abuse and Neglect of Children in Evolutionary Perspective." In R. D. Alexander and D. W. Tinkle (Eds.), *Natural Selection and Social Behavior: Recent Research and New Theory.* New York: Chiron Press, 1980b.

Dickemann, M. "Demographic Consequences of Infanticide in Man." *Annual Review of Ecology and Systematics,* 1975, *6,* 107-137.

Dickemann, M. "The Ecology of Mating Systems in Hypergynous Dowry Societies." *Social Science Information,* 1979, *18* (2), 163-195.

Dickemann, M. "Paternal Confidence and Dowry Competition: A Biocultural Analysis of Purdah." In R. D. Alexander and D. W. Tinkle (Eds.), *Natural Selection and Social Behavior: Recent Research and New Theory.* New York: Chiron Press, 1980.

Draper, P. "Social and Economic Constraints on Child Life among the !Kung." In R. B. Lee and I. DeVore (Eds.), *Kalahari Hunter-Gatherers.* Cambridge, Mass.: Harvard University Press, 1976.

Drotar, D., Baskiewicz, A., Irvin, N., Kennell, J., and Klaus, M. "The Adaptation of Parents to the Birth of an Infant with a Congenital Malformation: A Hypothetical Model." *Pediatrics,* 1975, *56,* 710-717.

Duberman, L. *The Reconstituted Family: A Study of Remarried Couples and Their Children.* Chicago: Nelson-Hall, 1975.

Erickson, C. J., and Zenone, P. G. "Courtship Differences in Male Ring Doves: Avoidance of Cuckoldry?" *Science,* 1976, *192,* 1353-1354.

Fergusson, D. M., Fleming, J., and O'Neill, D. P. *Child Abuse in New Zealand.* Wellington: Government of New Zealand Printer, 1972.

Firth, R. W. *We, the Tikopia: A Sociological Study of Kinship in Primitive Polynesia.* London: Allen & Unwin, 1936.

Fisher, R. A. *The Genetical Theory of Natural Selection.* (2nd ed.). New York: Dover, 1958.

Fletcher, J. "Attitudes toward Defective Newborns." *Hastings Center Studies,* 1974, *2,* 21-32.

Garbarino, J. "A Preliminary Study of Socioeconomic Stress on Mothers." *Child Development,* 1976, *47,* 178-185.

Gowaty, P. A. "The Experimenter as Iago? Aggression of Eastern Bluebirds *(Sialia Sialis)* to Conspecific Intruders During the Nesting Cycle." Paper presented at Animal Behavior Society, New Orleans, Louisiana, June 10-15, 1979.

Granzberg, G. "Twin Infanticide — A Cross-Cultural Test of a Materialistic Explanation." *Ethos,* 1973, *1,* 405-412.

Greig-Smith, P. W. "Parental Investment in Nest Defence by Stonechats *(Saxicola Torquata)*." *Animal Behaviour,* 1980, *28,* 604-619.

Hamilton, W. D. "The Evolution of Social Behavior, 1 and 2." *Journal of Theoretical Biology,* 1964, *7,* 1-52.

Hamilton, W. D. "Extraordinary Sex Ratios." *Science,* 1967, *156,* 477-488.

Harpending, H. "Regional Variation in !Kung Populations." In R. B. Lee and I. DeVore (Eds.), *Kalahari Hunter-Gatherers.* Cambridge, Mass.: Harvard University Press, 1976.

Hartung, J. "On Natural Selection and the Inheritance of Wealth." *Current Anthropology,* 1976, *17,* 607-622.

Howe, H. F. "Sex-Ratio and Adjustments in the Common Grackle." *Science,* 1977, *198,* 744-746.

Howell, N. "The Population of the Dobe Area !Kung." In R. B. Lee and I. DeVore (Eds.), *Kalahari Hunter-Gatherers.* Cambridge, Mass.: Harvard University Press, 1976.

Howell, N. *Demography of the Dobe !Kung.* New York: Academic Press, 1979.

Hrdy, S. B. "Infanticide among Animals: A Review, Classification, and Examination of the Implications for the Reproductive Strategies of Females. *Ethology and Sociobiology,* 1979, *1,* 13–40.

Kennell, J. H., Trause, M. A., and Klaus, M. H. "Evidence for a Sensitive Period in the Human Mother." In CIBA Foundation Symposium 33 *Parent-Infant Interaction.* Amsterdam: Elsevier-Excerpta Medica-North Holland, 1975.

Klaus, M. H., and Kennell, J. H. *Maternal-Infant Bonding.* St. Louis, Mo.: C. B. Mosby, 1976.

Klaus, M. H., Trause, M. A., and Kennell, J. H. "Does Human Maternal Behavior after Delivery Show a Characteristic Pattern?" In CIBA Foundation Symposium 33 *Parent-Infant Interaction.* Amsterdam: Elsevier-Excerpta Medica-North Holland, 1975.

Konner, M J. "Maternal Care, Infant Behavior, and Development among the !Kung." In R. B. Lee and I. DeVore (Eds.), *Kalahari Hunter-Gatherers.* Cambridge, Mass.: Harvard University Press, 1976.

Konner, M. "Infancy among the Kalahari Desert San." In P. H. Leiderman, S. R. Tulkin, and A. Rosenfeld (Eds.), *Culture and Infancy.* New York: Academic Press, 1977.

Konner, M., and Worthman, C. "Nursing Frequency, Gonadal Function, and Birth Spacing among !Kung Hunter-Gatherers." *Science,* 1980, *207,* 788–791.

Kurland, J. A. "Paternity, Mother's Brother, and Human Sociality." In N. A. Chagnon and W. Irons (Eds.), *Evolutionary Biology and Human Social Behavior: An Anthropological Perspective.* North Scituate, Mass.: Duxbury Press, 1979.

Lagacé, R. O. *Nature and Use of the HRAF Files. A Research and Teaching Guide.* New Haven, Conn.: Human Relations Area Files, 1974.

Langer, W. "Infanticide: A Historical Survey." *History of Childhood Quarterly,* 1974, *1,* 353–365.

Lawick-Goodall, J. van. *In the Shadow of Man.* London: Book Club Associates, 1971.

Lee, R. B., and DeVore, I. *Kalahari Hunter-Gatherers.* Cambridge, Mass.: Harvard University Press, 1976.

Lenington, S. "Child Abuse and Evolutionary Models for Human Behavior." Unpublished manuscript, University of Chicago, 1979.

Lewontin, R. C. "Sociobiology as an Adaptationist Program." *Behavioral Science,* 1979, *24,* 5–14.

Lindburg, D. G. "The Rhesus Monkey in North India: An Ecological and Behavioral Study." In L. A. Rosenblum (Ed.), *Primate Behavior: Development in Field and Laboratory Research.* Vol. 2. New York: Academic Press, 1971.

Lozoff, B., and Brittenham, G. "Infant Care: Cache or Carry." *Journal of Pediatrics,* 1979, *95,* 478–483.

Lozoff, B., Brittenham, C. M., Trause, M. A., Kennell, J. H., and Klaus, M. H. "The Mother-Newborn Relationship: Limits of Adaptability." *Journal of Pediatrics,* 1977, *91,* 1–12.

Lynch, M. A. "Ill-Health and Child Abuse." *The Lancet,* 1975, *2,* 317–319.

MacFarland, D. J. "Decision-Making in Animals." *Nature,* 1977, *269,* 15–21.

Martin, P. "Marital Breakdown in Families of Patients with Spina Bifida Cystica." *Developmental Medicine and Child Neurology,* 1975, *17,* 757–764.

O'Connor, S., Vietze, P. M., Hopkins, J. B., and Altemeier, W. A. "Postpartum Extended Mother-Infant Contact: Subsequent Mothering and Child Health." *Pediatric Research,* 1977, *11,* 380.

O'Connor, S., Vietze, P. M., Sherrod, K. B., Sandler, H. M., and Altemeier, W. A.

"Reduced Incidence of Parenting Disorders Following Rooming-In." Unpublished manuscript, Nashville General Hospital, 1979.

Pelton, L. H. "Child Abuse and Neglect: The Myth of Classlessness." *American Journal of Orthopsychiatry,* 1978, *48,* 608–617.

Pianka, E. R., and Parker, W. S. "Age-Specific Reproductive Tactics." *American Naturalist,* 1975, *109,* 453–464.

Pierotti, R. "Spite and Altruism in Gulls." *American Naturalist,* 1980, *115,* 290–300.

Power, H. W. "Mountain Bluebirds: Experimental Evidence Against Altruism." *Science,* 1975, *189,* 142–143.

Richards, M. P. M. "Possible Effects of Early Separation on Later Development of Children: A Review." In F. S. W. Brimblecombe, M. P. M. Richards, and N. C. R. Roberton (Eds.), *Separation and Special-care Baby Units.* Philadelphia: Lippincott, 1978.

Safilios-Rothschild, C. "'Honour' Crimes in Contemporary Greece." *British Journal of Sociology,* 1969, *29,* 205–218.

Stearns, S. C. "Life-history Tactics: A Review of the Ideas." *Quarterly Review of Biology,* 1976, *51,* 3–47.

Sugarman, M. "Paranatal Influences on Maternal-Infant Attachment." *American Journal of Orthopsychiatry,* 1977, *47,* 407–421.

Symons, D. *The Evolution of Human Sexuality.* New York: Oxford University Press, 1979.

Tew, B. J., Payne, H., and Laurence, K. M. "Must a Family with a Handicapped Child Be a Handicapped Family?" *Developmental Medicine and Child Neurology,* 1974, *16,* (supplement 32), 95–98.

Thomas, M. P. "Child Abuse and Neglect." Part 1: "Historical Overview, Legal Matrix, and Social Perspectives." *North Carolina Law Review,* 1972, *50,* 293–349.

Trivers, R. L. "Parental Investment and Sexual Selection." In B. Campbell (Ed.), *Sexual Selection and the Descent of Man 1871–1971.* Chicago: Aldine, 1972.

Trivers, R. L. "Parent-Offspring Conflict." *American Zoologist,* 1974, *14,* 249–264.

Trivers, R. L., and Willard, D. E. "Natural Selection of Parental Ability to Vary the Sex Ratio of Offspring." *Science,* 1973, *179,* 90–92.

Versterdal, J. "Psychological Mechanisms in Child-Abusing Parents." In J. M. Ekelaar and S. N. Katz (Eds.), *Family Violence: An International and Interdisciplinary Study.* Toronto: Butterworths, 1978.

Williams, G. C. *Adaptation and Natural Selection.* Princeton, N.J.: Princeton University Press, 1966.

Wilson, M. I., Daly, M., and Weghorst, S. J. "Household Composition and the Risk of Child Abuse and Neglect." *Journal of Biosocial Science,* 1980, *12* (3), 333–340.

Wilson, M. I., Daly, M., and Weghorst, S. J. "Differential Maltreatment of Girls and Boys." *Victimology: An International Journal,* in press.

Zenone, P. G. "Resident Male Response to Conspecific Intrusion during the Breeding Cycle of the Ring Dove *(Streptopelia Risoria)."* Paper presented at Animal Behavior Society, Fort Collins, Colorado, June 9–13, 1980.

Martin Daly and Margo Wilson are in the Department of Psychology at McMaster University, Hamilton, Ontario, Canada, where their research concerns social behavior and reproductive strategies in kangaroo rats, deer mice, and people.

Index

New Directions Quarterly Sourcebooks

New Directions for Child Development is one of several distinct series of quarterly sourcebooks published by Jossey-Bass. The sourcebooks in each series are designed to serve both as *convenient compendiums* of the latest knowledge and practical experience on their topics and as *long-life reference tools*.

One-year, four-sourcebook subscriptions for each series cost $18 for individuals (when paid by personal check) and $30 for institutions, libraries, and agencies. Single copies of earlier sourcebooks are available at $6.95 each *prepaid* (or $7.95 each when *billed*).

A complete listing is given below of current and past sourcebooks in the *New Directions for Child Development* series. The titles and editors-in-chief of the other series are also listed. To subscribe, or to receive further information, write: New Directions Subscriptions, Jossey-Bass Inc., Publishers, 433 California Street, San Francisco, California 94104.

New Directions for Child Development
William Damon, Editor-in-Chief
1978–1979:   1. *Social Cognition,* William Damon
                2. *Moral Development,* William Damon
                3. *Early Symbolization,* Howard Gardner, Dennie Wolf
                4. *Social Interaction and Communication During Infancy,* Ina C. Uzgiris
1979–1980:   5. *Intellectual Development Beyond Childhood,* Deanna Kuhn
                6. *Fact, Fiction, and Fantasy in Childhood,* Ellen Winner, Howard Gardner
                7. *Clinical-Developmental Psychology,* Robert L. Selman, Regina Yando
                8. *Anthropological Perspectives on Child Development,* Charles M. Super, Sara Harkness
1980–1981:   9. *Children's Play,* Kenneth H. Rubin
             10. *Children's Memory,* Marion Perlmutter

New Directions for College Learning Assistance
Kurt V. Lauridsen, Editor-in-Chief

New Directions for Community Colleges
Arthur M. Cohen, Editor-in-Chief
Florence B. Brawer, Associate Editor

New Directions for Continuing Education
Alan B. Knox, Editor-in-Chief

New Directions for Exceptional Children
James J. Gallagher, Editor-in-Chief

New Directions for Experiential Learning
Pamela J. Tate, Editor-in-Chief
Morris T. Keeton, Consulting Editor

New Directions for Higher Education
JB Lon Hefferlin, Editor-in-Chief

New Directions for Institutional Advancement
A. Westley Rowland, Editor-in-Chief

New Directions for Institutional Research
Marvin W. Peterson, Editor-in-Chief

New Directions for Mental Health Services
H. Richard Lamb, Editor-in-Chief

New Directions for Methodology of Social and Behavioral Science
Donald W. Fiske, Editor-in-Chief

New Directions for Program Evaluation
Scarvia B. Anderson, Editor-in-Chief

New Directions for Student Services
Ursula Delworth and Gary R. Hanson, Editors-in-Chief

New Directions for Teaching and Learning
Kenneth E. Eble and John F. Noonan, Editors-in-Chief

New Directions for Testing and Measurement
William B. Schrader, Editor-in-Chief